The
African Fiction

The African Fiction

edited by

SHYAM S. AGARWALLA

PRESTIGE

Published by
PRESTIGE BOOKS
3/28, East Patel Nagar
New Delhi 110 008

2000

ISBN: 81-7551-071-4

Composed by Vivek Mathur, Delhi 110 005
Printed by Dhawan Industries Offset, New Delhi 110 028

Contents

The African Novel: New Insights

Women's Voices

Chinua Achebe

Contributors

G.D. BARCHE	S.S.V.P.S's Arts and Commerce College, Dhule
USHA BHATNAGAR	S.P.M. College, University of Delhi
TERRY COLLITS	University of Melbourne, Australia
STEPHEN CRISWELL	Louisiana, USA
SUREKHA DANGWAL	Dayanand University, Rohtak
FREDERICK HALE	Minnesota, U.S.A.
V.T. GIRDHARI	People's College, Nanded
B. INDIRA	Regional Engineering College, Visakhapatnam
S. INDIRA	Dr. L.B. College, Visakhapatnam
AYESHA IRFAN	Jamia Millia Islamia, New Delhi
S.A. KHAYYOOM	S.K. University, Anantapur
AMINA KISHORE	A.M.U., Aligarh
YASHODA RAMAMOORTHY	Pune. Formerly Professor of English in Africa
R.M.V. RAGHAVENDRA RAO	Bhavan's New Science, Arts & Commerce College, Hyderabad
INDRASENA REDDY	Kakatiya University, Warangal
K. VENKATA REDDY	S.K. University, Anantapur
SHOBHA SHINDE	Jai Hind College, Dhule
G. SUDHAKAR	Kakatiya University, Warangal
ANDRE H. TOLOFON	Universite Omar Bongo, Liberville
P.D. TRIPATHI	University of Texas, Austin

Time and Historic Sense in the Commonwealth Novel with Special Reference to India and Africa

AMINA KISHORE

The two bases of fictional art have been considered to be temporality and spatiality. Time is the medium of the narrative art. This is not difficult to argue, since all literature is, after all, a temporal art. When it comes to fiction, one might say that the rhythm of the novel is essentially the rhythm of time: events, movements, beginnings, closures—and all such fictional materials are moulded and contained by Time.

Though fictional narrative is bound by events in time, the life of the narrative depends on the writer's presentation of the events in significant patterns or associations. These significant patterns impose implicit persuasion on the reader until the events become real in his/her experience. Once those events become events in our inner world, the time-order of the narrated events ceases to be significant. There is, one can say, a fusion of time elements, i.e., the author-ordered time of the narrated event and the reader's experiential time become one. The dualities of Time-experience and events in time are suggested by many writers. Theorists like Hans Meyer Hoff have explored the factor of Time in literature. Ajneya in his *A Sense of Time* (OUP) refers to self-conscious projection of time in fictional works like *Tristram Shandy* by Laurence Sterne.

The treatment of time in literature is very different from the logical scientific construct of Time. The Time which literature deals with is, actually, Time in experience. The measurement, order and duration and even direction of Time may be bent to the yardstick of an experiential metric by the literary artist.

The conventional beginnings of the oral narrative, on which all earlier, conventional fiction models itself, operated within a loose temporal and spatial orientation. The 'Once upon a time there lived a king' kind of a beginning suggests a very unique dimension of Time. This special dimension of Time is different from the clock-hour-calendar-day-month-year time. It is unhistoric and indeterminate; yet it is real because it operates within its own laws of probability and possibility.

The 'Once upon a time there was a king' pattern is interestingly taken up by thoroughly modern novelists like Hemingway. The beginning of *A Farewell to Arms*—'The summer of that year we lived in a house'—the indefinite article and the vaguely indicative 'that' fix the narrative in a timeless, spaceless dimension. This is persuasive invitation to shed the bindings of ordinary experience and move into an unprejudicial state of mind. As Vatsyayan says, "Men of all ages are always ready for the suspension of disbelief if the consequences are pleasurable" or exciting. The devices of timelessness render narrative time fluid or compressed and this keeps alive the interest of the reader by allowing him freedom to use his imagination in comprehending the time dimension.

According to Bergson, "Time is the immediate datum of consciousness." By binding the fictional narrative in the confines of Time, the fictionist attempts to accord immediate realism to the narrative. The reading of fiction-text with an eye on the author's time-management may give a great insight into the author's intended foregroundings of thematic materials. In other words, the greater the narrative time expended on presenting an event in time, the more it is an indication of the fact that the author wishes to achieve reader-empathy through persuasive verbiage.

A novel like Anand's *Untouchable* is 180 pages long and covers a day in Bakha's life. On the other hand, a moment in a fictional character's consciousness may take many pages. It is this personal metric that Virginia Woolf refers to in *Orlando*: "An hour, once it lodges in the queer element of the human spirit, may be stretched to 50 or 100 times in clock length; on the other hand, an hour may be actually represented by the timepiece of the mind by one second." In Ayi Kwei Armah's *Two Thousand Seasons*, the collective voice 'we' of the narrators determines its own fluid time frame so that the "recapitulating of 2000 seasons, or one millennium" becomes possible. Thus literature, and fiction especially, transcends ordinary modalities of Time. Novelists like Joyce, Woolf, Ghosh, Raja Rao and Rushdie, are constantly stretching the limits of the fictional genre by defying the temporal restrictions which the 'realistic' tradition imposes on their art.

The play with the temporal order, however, is merely a structuring of the events and an arbitrary ordering of sequentiality. The author selects the patterns in which he wishes to mould the consciousness of his readers. The inherent and actual sequentiality of the event does not undergo any change. It cannot; just as the historic direction of Time movement and event cannot really change. The significance of the meaning of the author lies in two things: (a) The chosen events in time—(the narrative does choose and select, though it pretends to tell 'All'); and (b) The chosen sequence (whether ordered or disordered). Any ambiguity that may arise out of such arbitrariness is smoothed over by the apparent sequentiality of the narrative idiom which lives by its linguistic base—through devices like anaphora, referentiality, repetition and refrain.

Modern fiction achieves the fusion of present time and the past (i.e. the narrative and narrated times) through various techniques. Most of these techniques are appropriated by these modern writers from the socio-cultural, philosophical milieus to which they are native. For example, most western writers take a linear view of time while the oriental cyclic view of time affects the time-view of most of the Asian writers. The recti-linear view of historic time generally held by the African writer is the product of the combined influence of Christianity, Islam and Marxism on African thought. These three philosophies are linked with the notion of history as progressive fulfilment of Destiny, with each event only a stage in the path of the ultimate goal. Other conventional models for explaining human time which have been exploited by writers are the alternating, undulating and spiral movements. These are symbolically represented through the seasons, river, pendulum and fan and many other motifs in literary texts. Narrative modes like dream, journey, memory also help to foreground a dimension of consciousness which is free of the constraints of time and space.

Increasing interest of the novelists in aspects of Time has also given a rise to an interest in myth. Myth has been described as a "timeless schema" (Thomas Mann) or "timeless prototype." Myths keep alive the link between the past and the present alive by suggesting repetitions through highly charged symbols. The logical continuity may not be there but a similarity of design suggests parallels.

The first manifestation of the temporal factor in fiction, then, is the artistic admixing of the dual patterns of narrated Time and narrative time. Fictive Time is the result of this amalgam. The other aspect of Time in a novel is the dimension of history or an attachment to the past. Whatever the date of the narrated event may be, the moment of narration is always one step ahead in time. The eye of the narrator has seen it happen. It is history which is narrated. The distance which this factor creates is very important. It gives to fiction the status of referential, myth-like super-text. This implied distance between event and narration of event suggests possibilities of interpretive assimilation and evaluations.

Fictional idiom is the idiom of retrospection. Its reflexive reference helps to give a telescoped perception of time. In a way time is scaled to the perceptive capacity of the human mind. Even in the novels which are futuristic in terms of narrated event, or in novels which project abstract, imaginary, capsuled time-blocks, and tone of the narrative is past-bound. The novel, like biography and autobiography, uses the memory pattern and historic data base.

Traditional fiction, with its realistic dimension, claimed continuous access to history, "seducing us, by its narrative design, into identifying with the individual experience of living through history." In the past few decades, the interest in the use of historical material and the concept of history has undergone a change. Now-a-days, it is no more 'historical mimicry' which is important but the underlying choice of moments of history. Good examples of this new vision of history are Amitav Ghosh's *In an Antique Land, The Shadow Lines*, O.V. Vijayan's *History of the Kazaks* and Armah's *Two Thousand Seasons.* The reader is pressurized (albeit subtly) to read into the way in which history is presented, to hear the undertones—adulatory, ironic, referential, etc. That alone will explicate the thematic preoccupation of the novelists. E.M. Forster's use of the historic moment and the historic ethos is not merely a realistic prop—it is an ironic history (or historical irony?) which in its own turn reveals the author's insight into the follies of the Power Politics. Of course the pleasures of Forster's novels lie in the novelist's detachment and the non-partisan role as an interpreter. But the deeper significance of such a novel as *A Passage to India* lies in its perspicacity, its prophecy.

The Commonwealth novelist needs individual attention at this juncture of my paper. The postcolonial Commonwealth novelist is as yet too embroiled in the red-hot colonization issue to have learned to become totally objective in his use of history besides other issues. But the capacity for self-directed humour, irony and clear-sighted criticism as one finds in the novels of Mulk Raj Anand, Chinua Achebe, Wole Soyinka and Desani is a sign of the maturity of the new literatures; so also is the high degree of introspective philosophic skepticism of Rao. Lately writers like Ghosh and Armah have shown how the causes for hope and despair have to be searched for and found in the backwaters of the history of human consciousness and not in the frontal streams of recorded or recordable history. This understanding of the commonwealth novel will help to release fictional evolution from fixed grooves like postcolonial discourse, or postmodern ideology.

The hazards of reading a novel in terms of the history it contains are many. The text could easily come under fire for laxity in veracity and be subject to charges of 'misinterpretation' of fact. As 'fictionalized fact,' the text could become a puzzle for a reader since the decision as to where history ends and fiction begins can also become problematic. Rushdie's fate is a good example of this hazard.

Critical readership has to be wary of making hasty pronouncements. Surface readings and shallow interpretations are the bane of the artist's will to survive and his ultimate goal of making 'connections.' Critical misreadings of the Commonwealth novels are responsible for labelling of the Indian and African novels. The usual responses to these novels are obvious in the topics of research and critical papers. These invariably look for East-West encounters, Gandhian influence, British Raj motifs and neo-, anti-, postcolonialism, postcolonial discourse etc. Read carefully, the historic background can be seen to be merely a mode of crystallization of the significant moments of man's journey in experiential time. The fused patterns of the macro-history of a nation (a temporal-spatial verity) with individual (micro) history, result in the foregrounding of the essential Truth of the artist's vision—his conception of the human condition, boundless and limitless both temporally and spatially.

The fictional form is a suitable form for the expression of this conception of history since the novel contains the scope of beginning at no real beginning and ending at no real end. This "faking" is commensurate with the game of historical time that the novel plays; so that narrative and narrated Time become metaphors for the time-experience. And Time experience, one must reiterate, is end product of an exposure to a narrative work.

The serious Commonwealth novelist is trying to understand himself in terms of history, biography, autobiography, tradition, and a much-riddled time concept. The western novel examines the conflict between linear structure/narrative in time and the timeless concept of subjective experience in time, attempting to relate the opposed notions of private time and historic or public time.

The traditions of India and Africa provide a possibility of moving in a 'timeless' dimension of experience where past, present and future are merged into one. According to these traditions, the very concept of

Time is touched with illusoriness. All 'reality' is touched with 'unreality'— mithya. Sequentiality and causality are the facades that human logic creates to explain an otherwise beyond logic, irrational concept.

General critical strain which tries to 'discover' tragic undertones in the Commonwealth novelist's quest for identity or search for roots exhibits a lack of understanding of the new literatures which are twice-born. Contrary to the usual western view, the Indian and African writers are not 'separated' from their past nor are they traumatized by any alienating distance from their traditions. The use of the historic past generally implies a re-appraisal of traditions and attempts to adjust it to a functionally viable proposition for twentieth century living. As S.C. Harrex says, the Indian writer's philosophic make up is supported by his historical sense, i.e., it is not just a metaphysical and spiritual world view but a vision of ideal humanity. This sense of tradition is perhaps more stable and more steadily ingrained in the Indian writer than in the comparatively more traumatized African writers. As T.S. Eliot says in "Tradition and the Individual Talent": "The historical sense involves a perception, not only of the pastness of the past, but of its presence; the historical sense compels a man to write not merely with his own generation in his bones, but with a feeling that the whole of the literature of Europe from Homer and within it, the whole of the literature of his own country has a simultaneous order. This historical sense, which is a sense of the timeless and of the temporal together, is what makes a writer traditional. And it is at the same time what makes a writer most acutely conscious of his place in time, of his own contemporaneity."

The historical sense as perceived by the writers from Africa and Asia is clearly different from Eliot's implied case-studies of the European sensibility. The writers of the new nations differ from each other and so do individual writers of the same nations. The "sense of the timeless as well as the temporal" as Eliot appreciates in *Four Quartets* is ingrained in the Eastern cultural traditions much more than it is in the tradition of "the literature from Europe from Homer." But Eliot's definition of tradition holds quite true in the cases of Armah and Raja Rao. The historic sense in many of the postcolonial Commonwealth novels continues to possess the flavour of myth to which both India and Africa are native.

For all the intensity and past-bound nature of the African novel in English, the African novelist is not a pensive creature of the past. He is an artist historian. The period of colonialism is generally seen by him as a temporary check in the fulfilment of African destiny. Major African writers are openly critical of a mindless and regressive past for mere evocative value. Faith in the past comes out as a central concern in African novels. But it is only artistic faith. The African writer does not wish to achieve the past itself but he does long for an achievement of a memory of the past.

To conclude, the concerns of the African writers are much more complex than mere obsession with the past or a preoccupation with the present. The writer in Africa is looking at the "pre-colonial past as a prelude and the colonial past as a discordant interlude" which will ultimately conclude in a "harmony to the historical experience of the race at the end of time."

The final note in the Commonwealth novels is one of reconciliation, a transcendence of social self and a recovery of the essential Human Self. In this measure, the "historical sense" becomes a mode of reaffirmation of the human spirit.

Gabriel Okara's *The Voice*: An African Quest in the Face of Colonialism

YASHODA RAMAMOORTHY

Colonialism in African countries thrived on the Eurocentric notions about history and civilizations according to which the Africans had no past and no history and so, they were child-like or primitive. This faulty, self-righteous and arrogant attitude along with the imposition of Christianity, Western education and consequently a total set of new values, created a tremendous amount of pressure and conflict on the minds of the Africans. That is why when the early generation of the writers started expressing themselves, their primary task was two-fold. Firstly, to inform the outside world about Africa's past and culture, and secondly to restore the lost confidence in the African himself. Achebe views the writer as a teacher. Ngugi wa Thiong'o goes a step further and views the writer not only as a teacher but also as a maker of revolutions. In their novels and through them, Achebe and Ngugi recreate the African past by making use of the myths, legends and proverbs from their respective societies. Sometimes even the actual historical happenings are interwoven in their novels. Camara Laye, Wole Soyinka and others too have written about the clashing cultures in their own inimicable ways in their works.

But there are some writers who have tried to present the over-all African philosophy. This is found in different degrees in Amos Tutuola's *Palm Wine Drinkard*, Camara Laye's *Radiance of the King* (originally in French) and Gabriel Okara's *The Voice* and in Okot p'Bitek's *Song of Lawino* (although it is in poetry form). *Palm Wine Drinkard* is essentially a bold stylistic experimentation through which the novelist's intention seems to be the projection of a rich African oral narrative tradition as against the Western literary forms, particularly the novel, which many writers on the continent were adopting. Whereas Camara Laye's *Radiance of the King* exposes the penury of the White man's culture which depends mainly on material gains and success by juxtaposing it with a vibrant and unfathomable African philosophy in the complex plot of the novel. Symbolically the White character Clarence is depicted as a beggar!

Gabriel Okara's *The Voice* (incidentally the only novel from the West African poet) comes out with a more unified presentation of what is at the core of African philosophy—grappling with the abstract—than in the above-mentioned novels. Here the abstract or the unseen is not in a supernatural way but as a totality of human existence as understood in African thinking. Man's role and place not only in the society but in the universe. Not only here and now but in eternity. What was implied in the novels of Joseph Conrad, a hidden bright spot in *Heart of Darkness* is elaborated here with more ease and a better authenticity. Conrad's Kurtz in *Heart of Darkness* is afraid of speaking the truth that the so-called savages were better than the Europeans, and throughout he is made to be misunderstood, as Conrad knew at that time, the truth would not be acceptable as he was writing in the heyday of colonialism.

The Voice, although limited in its theme, encompasses within its scope a variety of issues that have troubled the African novelist since the beginning of this century. Some of these are: clash of cultures, identity crisis and evils of capitalism such as corruption and prostitution etc. But Okara views these issues in a broader perspective without entering into polemics as some writers have done. Without dwelling upon these broad issues, Okara touches upon the core i.e., man's tryst with destiny, or, his quest for the meaning of life. *The Voice* is a political parable and so the plot is kept at its minimum. The theme is an individual's crusade in the face of corruption in neo-colonial Nigeria. But the crusade is in the form of introvertion, a quest, not in the form of external militancy. It is the quest for the meaning of life, or simply *it* as it is referred to in the novel: for a considerable length in the novel, *it* is not explained. The thin outlines of the plot revolve round Okolo of Amatu, an Ijaw speaking village in Nigeria. On the surface of it, the story is very simple. The people of Amatu think that Okolo has gone mad, due to his strange behaviour. His main fault is that he thinks differently from others and so he doesn't fall into their set pattern of behaviour. The real reason however is that the people in position are scared of Okolo as they see a 'method in his madness' and a threat to their snug and conceitful stand in grappling with power. When the elders in Amatu, particularly Izongo, visualise clearly this threat to their own position in Okolo's wisdom, they decide to send him into exile after making a last appeal to him to change and fall into the pattern—their pattern. But even their last appeal does not influence him to change as he has seen the face of truth and now his conscience will not permit him to reject the earlier position he has taken with regard to present-day social evils. So he accepts his lot and leaves for Sologa (an imaginary neighbouring country) in a boat. This part of the narrative describing the boat journey emerges as the liveliest in the whole work and is indeed the mainstay of the novel. The common folk of Nigeria (or for that matter even of West Africa), 'the White man's food-cooker,' the engine driver, the fat mother-in-law and her comely daughter-in-law with their petty boastful achievements and their personal Gods whom every one invokes differently in the times of crisis such as torrential rains during the journey, not only shed light on the life in Nigeria but also prevent the novel from falling into a total allegorical rendering. The novelist's keen sense of observation and a sense of humour albeit in a controlled way since it is essentially of a tragedy come to the forefront here. On the boat, during the journey also, Okolo is misunderstood for having given shelter to a young bride under his raincoat when it rains heavily. The girl's would-be mother-in-law charges him with immodest behaviour. The silence which he kept during earlier part of the journey due to the heavy thing weighing him down—his existential problem—is misunderstood as roguery. Misfortune follows him even to Sologa since the word has already reached there about his madness. Although persons like eating-house owner take to him kindly, all advise him to give up his search for *it*. The thread of allegory is resumed and the big political scenarios and the personalities are merely alluded to in this part of the novel. The neo-colonial situation which other novelists such as Ngugi wa Thiong'o have taken pains to describe in endless pages, is presented by Okara in only a few glimpses through the persons like The Big Man (the political leader or minister), the police, the white man helping the 'big man'—the real string puller—in this part of the novel. It is almost like a pageant. To his horror, Okolo sees unmentionable things in Sologa. Like skeletons in the big leader's house, or the police man's disappearance from the scene when Okolo talks about this. The heartless city and helpless people are best summed up by Okolo:

> Okolo waited and waited for the constable but the constable did not return. He stood there and waited with the crowd passing him by, but Okolo even the constable's shadow did not see. So to the inside of Sologa of the Big One he walked with each step begging

> the ground. So Okolo walked in Sologa of the Big One passing frustrated eyes, ground-looking eyes, harlot's eyes, nothing-looking eyes, hot eyes, cold eyes, bruised eyes, despairing eyes, nothing-caring eyes, grabbing eyes, dust-filled eyes, aping eyes.[1]

The corruption at high places combined with political ambitions and ruthless pirations of the big people have made the common man helpless and puppet-like. The vicious and fear clamped atmosphere of Sologa is best summed up in the outlines, without names; the leader is just the Big One (it does not matter who he is). The psychophants and the spies in the system are the dummy like 'listeners.' And the passing flow of humanity in its helplessness is best described in the above passage. In this chapter the allegory mode in the narration overtakes and only the essentials are given, raising the problem from its local level to universal plane. Just as good can be all-pervasive, evil also can be universal. And when this happens, life is reduced to a mechanical pattern and human beings are turned soulless. It is not that others besides Okolo have not realised this in Sologa, or that they are least bothered. They are only practical when Okolo is heroic! The eating-house owner's practical advice and also that of his well wisher Teibewoi earlier in the novel point to this. The eating-house owner says: "Do not think any more, my man. The people who have the sweetest insides are the think nothing people and we here try to be like them. Like logs in the river we float and go whither the current commands and nothing enters our insides to turn the sweetness into bitterness, so my man, here stay and be one of us." (84)

There is not much difference between one place and another in a neo-colonial situation. Although his position is like that of a person caught between the devil and the deep sea, he opts to follow his conscience and not run away, but to return to his land of birth even if it means certain death. His umbilical cord is buried there, in his village and he has to hear its call. (74, 97) This impending tragedy and Okolo's unswerving belief in himself, and in the ancestral voice of his father which has been a guiding force and which has been telling him to do 'the straight thing,' (106) even if it means poverty, are depicted with an excellent economy of movements and narration. Okolo's return journey is less eventful and more ponderous in the thought process he undergoes. He has learnt lessons, both at personal as well as at social levels and his predicament in the face of antagonistic societal forces become clearer to him. His existential problem which is not purely ontological and the stand he has to take with regard to his society come out in a crystal clear fashion in the following passage:

> Yes, each one has a meaning of life to himself. And that is perhaps the root of the conflict. No one can enter another's inside. You try to enter and you are kicked out at the door. You allow another to enter your inside and see everything in it, you are regarded as one without a chest or as one who nothing knows. . . . Maybe he is wrong. There may be only one meaning in life and everybody is just groping along in their various ways to achieve it like religion—Christians, Moslems, Animists—all trying to reach God in their various ways. What is he himself trying to reach? For him it has no name. Names bring divisions and divisions, strife. So let it be without a name; let it be nameless . . .
>
> So Okolo for three days and three nights sitting with his knees drawn up to his chin, talked in his inside and in the end agreed with his inside that everybody has or ought to have a purpose apart from bearing children and the sweetness of one's inside in the world is in the fulfilment of that purpose. The only hard thing, rather one of the two hard things is knowing your purpose is this world. The other which is harder, is not to corrupt it after knowing what your purpose is. As for him, his purpose he knows. He will keep it clean as a virgin sheet of white paper. And to keep it so clean, he will keep his inside as clean as the sky. (111-12)

The above passage serves as the best illustration of the unambiguous and straight way in which the existential problem is perceived not only by Okolo but also by the novelist, if for a moment we can agree that the novel is written with a purpose, and hence, the authorial voice.

Hamlet's analogy comes too close in this part of the novel to be missed since there is Ukule the cripple who along with Tuere, the so-called witch, has given moral support to Okolo is asked by both Okolo and Tuere to escape and survive in order to tell their tale to the world. Ukule in turn promises that he will do so and that Okolo's words will not die. But the analogy ends here. There are no Hamletian dilemmas in the novel. The strength of Okolo's moral conviction overpower the tragedy of his physical death. If anything, the Amatu society emerges as an imperfect and impoverished one and the question that Joan of Arc asks exasperatedly in his sadness in the concluding lines of George Bernard Shaw's *Saint Joan*: O God that madest this beautiful earth, when will it be ready to receive thy saints, How long, O God, how long!'[2] reverberates at the end of the novel. The authorial tone in the most moving description but without a trace of melodrama comes in the last paragraph:

> When day broke the following day it broke on a canoe aimlessly floating down the river. And in the canoe tied together back to back with their feet tied to the seats of canoe, were Okolo and Tuere. Down they floated from one bank of the river to the other like debris, carried by the current. Then the canoe was drawn into a whirlpool. It spun round and round and was slowly drawn into the core and finally disappeared. And the water rolled over the top and the river flowed smoothly over it as if nothing had happened. (127)

The Voice invites many interpretations. At the symbolic level, the name Okolo means voice when translated. It is the voice of this conscience, the voice of his forefathers and gradually Okolo stands for the inner voice, the collective conscience, of a society although all the others do not possess the clarity of vision or courage to see it. Nonetheless through the uneasiness felt by some minor characters like Tiri, Abadi or Tabeiwoi and the kind hotel-keeper of Sologa at Okolo's convictions pitted against prevalent malpractices in the society, the novelist makes it amply clear that Okolo was right and that it was not yet proper time for the people in general to realise it. There are also inner voices, at times conflicting, in the mind of Okolo. One strain of thinking prods his common sense asking him to save his skin but the other which is stronger and which he feels comes from his ancestors and so in a way belongs to the heritage to which he is born, strengthens his moral courage. Okolo is hoping against hope. He feels: "If the masses haven't got *it* he will create *it* in their insides. He will plant *it*, make *it* grow in spite of Izongo's destroying words. He will uproot the fear in their minds, kill the fear in their insides and plant *it*." (90)

The complex existential problem of an individual is simplified in this novel as a search for *it* which forms the theme of the novel. With the progress of the novel, the word *it* assumes a wide range of connotations. Okara purposely avoids to narrow it down to a particular quest undertaken by Okolo, or, to a particular meaning. Thus, sometimes *it* means soul or a strong moral character as when Okolo retorts Abadi, one of his opponents thus: "You have your M.A., Ph.D., but you have not got *it*." (44) The colonial edifice of pedagogic education comes down crumbling in the above sentence. We are reminded of Lawino's complaint in Okot p'Bitek's *Song of Lawino*:

> My husband's house
> Is a dark forest of books.[3]

Or,

> For all our young men
> Were finished in the forest,
> Their manhood was finished
> In the class-rooms,
> Their testicles
> Were smashed
> With large books! (191)

But at other times as in his stay in Sologa when the hotel-keeper exclaims that nobody has so far found *it,* (83-84) it means the meaning of life.

By doing this, Gabriel Okara opens a window on the abstruse nature and wide range of African spirituality and philosophy and of course, more importantly also on the hitherto unknown complex nature of African languages, for he has made use of Ijaw idiom in English very successfully. Their ancestors knew what was good and what was bad. No ambiguity was entertained in the ancient times about the moral code by which a society was governed. And even if times have changed, admittedly, what was held good once will always remain good. And so when Okolo sees immorality and corruption practised by his fellow beings in neo-colonial Nigeria in order to gain material success he is perturbed. People's bartering their souls for material success and gains is best summed up in the words of Tebeowei: "Everybody's inside is now filled with money, cars, and concrete houses and money is being scattered all around. If any falls at my feet, I stoop and pick it up. If I don't and kick it away, I will be called a know-nothing man and I will be kicked away." (50)

Where Ngugi wa Thing'o and Chinua Achebe have used the actual happenings and events in their fictional realism to deplore the prevailing situations in East and West Africa respectively, and have meticulously woven their novels around these happenings, Gabriel Okara has dealt with the problem at the entirely metaphorical or even metaphysical level, as if trying to assert that man's circumstances, social or historical, can be made, changed, and remade, but what matters most is the man himself, within these circumstances and fighting them if necessary, coming out strong in his character victorious or otherwise but never succumbing to lowly temptations, desires, or pressures once the realisation has dawned upon him about his true nature and his role in the society. This view poses a challenge not only to western materialism but also to Marxist insistence on the dialectical nature of materialism. Okolo says:

> All I want to do in my search . . . is to revitalise my flagging faith, faith in man, belief in something. . . . Belief and faith in that something we looked up to in times of sorrow and joy have all been taken away and in its stead what do we have? Nothing but a dried pool with only dead wood and skeleton leaves. And when you question they fear a tornado is going to blow down the beautiful houses they have built without foundations. (87-88)

This alternative viewpoint—an African viewpoint which is central to the novel—is presented in a most natural and befitting way by using English language the way an Ijaw-speaking person would use (presumably), which by implication refers to African way of looking at things. Their customs and beliefs, notions and concepts are skilfully woven into the texture of the novel. Even the tribal ways of dispensing justice is illustrated when Okolo is asked to take an oath to absolve him of the alleged sin he has committed by the elders in Sologa. The oath is taken by the elements of Nature, and once this is done, no iota of doubt remains in others about Okolo's innocence! Going back a little, the very use of the world *it*, a simple pronoun, asserts a positive note that in tribal African thinking such a thing, such a concept existed. In fact, it defies any attempt at translation!

Some very striking linguistic experimentations one comes across in the novel are: 'blacker than black night,' (16) 'you have been silent more than silence,' (65) 'It was rain time. So the river was full upto its brim and the water's power passed power.' (58) 'Silence passed silence.' (27) This kind of comparative mode is very often used in the novel to describe the ultimate, something beyond human imagination, quality which adds a peculiar charm to the narrative besides spelling out African imagination and speech patterns. Sometimes novel phrases like 'making people handsome day arrived,' (70) meaning evening, or, 'a girl with half ripe mango breasts and a sweet inside' (26) to sum up her youth, beauty and innocence, or at other place, 'with smile in his mouth

Okolo looked at Izongo' (46) suggesting victory or contempt.

Another typical device put to use by Okara is mimetic descriptions to assist the allegory mode of narration. These are amply evident in chapter two where people's helplessness, their oppressed state is brought to the surface in a puppetry fashion. When Izongo asks them to clap, they all clap, when he exhorts them to assent, they all nod their heads mechanically. The facelessness of the crowd, the masses is summed up a little later in Sologa scene where eyes are described as 'ground-looking eyes, harlot's eyes, nothing-looking eyes, despairing-eyes, grabbing-eyes.' (80) But the tone for this is set up right at the beginning of the novel where one of the messengers says: "As for me, . . . If the world turns this way I take it; if it turns another way I take it. Any way the world turns I take it with my hands. I like sleep and my wife and my one son, so I do not think." (25) This sums up the deplorable level of apathy to which people are sunk. Occasionally Okara uses rhetoric as a part of narrative:

> 'Han. . . . Amatu! In the town, are there people or not?'
>
> 'There are people!' cried the people at the tops of their voices and shaking their fists.
>
> 'Can we face any happening thing?'
>
> 'We can face anything,' answered the people with all the strength in their voices. (114)

Okara's frequent use of oral narrative tradition and his liberty with English language have in no way affected the art of the novel adversely. On the contrary, his experimentation of English in Ijaw idiom has not only fairly succeeded in enhancing the effectiveness of communication of the theme he had in mind, but has also opened up vast potentialities of such stylistic devices in overcoming the cultural barriers and limitations. There is perhaps no other way in which Okara could have squeezed the entire range of African thought abstract at so many levels without letting it to be cramped. A very good illustration of this is found towards the end of the novel when Tuere says to Ukule: "Then, nothing I will care, because whatever they do to Okolo is nothing, nothing!" (96-97) Physical death is not a tragedy here but a victory! If what Okolo held dear has roots somewhere else, in some one else's inside!

It should be remembered that Okara is basically a poet and so the metaphorical expressions, repeatedly punctuate his prose. His poetic sensibility is evident in not only the way in which he has used Ijaw idiom in English, but also in his perception, conceptualisation and a neat and skilfull execution of the theme in this highly artistic novel. Who else if not a poet could hold that words take roots and grow inside people who are awakened to truth?

NOTES

1. Gabriel Okara, *The Voice* (London: Heinemann Educational Books, 1977), p. 80.
2. George Bernard Shaw, *Saint Joan*, in *Complete Plays of Bernard Shaw* (London: Paul Hamlyn, 1965), p. 1009.
3. Okot p'Bitek *Song of Lawino and Song of Ocol* (Nairobi: East African Publishing House, 1972), p. 184.

The Decline of an Erstwhile Contemplative in T. Obinkaram Echewa's *The Land's Lord*

FREDERICK HALE

Few general themes in postcolonial Nigerian literature have enjoyed greater prominence than the disrupting impact of European civilization on the indigenous cultures of West Africa. In this regard many of the young nation's *litterateurs* have focused part of their attention on the cultural turmoil which propagators of Christianity have brought to both the religious and social life of ostensibly stable tribal societies. The renowned novelist Chinua Achebe, who in the 1950s and 1960s played a highly visible and internationally acclaimed role in launching and shaping the written literary tradition of Nigeria, had missionaries in his sights in such works as *Things Fall Apart* (1958) and *Arrow of God* (1964). Among his many colleagues in the formative era of postcolonial Nigerian fiction, Timothy Mofolorunso Aluko did likewise in *One Man, One Wife* (1959), as did Onuora Nzekwu in *Blade among the Boys* (1962) and Nkem Nwankwo in *Danda* (1964). Gabriel Okara did not deal directly with missionaries in his masterly short novel *The Voice* (1964) but therein gave readers a pithy treatment of the cultural and religious disorder which foreign purveyors of Christianity had wrought in Nigeria. In the international realm of analysis, scholarly attention has been perennially riveted on these and a few other writers of Nigerian fiction while generally paying little notice to many of the nation's other artists, some of whom have arguably treated implications of the intercultural religious clash with equal acumen.

One such writer is T. Obinkaram Echewa, who in his prize-winning novel of 1976, *The Land's Lord*, dealt more directly with the confrontations of Roman Catholicism and its missionaries with Igbo religion and its practitioners than any of his compatriots hitherto had or subsequently has done. When published in London and shortly thereafter in Connecticut, *The Land's Lord* received critical acclaim in West Africa, the United Kingdom and the United States of America. The well-known

American scholar Charles Larson found *The Land's Lord* virtually seamless and went so far as to aver that "everything in this superbly executed novel belongs here: every action, every speech, every question posed by the characters involved. Echewa's use of language is always fresh and often nothing short of spectacular."[1] The English-Speaking Union, moreover, awarded Echewa a major prize in 1977 for creating the previous year's best volume of *belles-lettres* in English by a non-native speaker of a language. Kolawole Ogungbesan of Ahmadu Bella University in Nigeria described *The Land's Lord* as "a successful portrait of spiritual conflict in the manner of classical tragedy."[2] Meanwhile, Eustace Palmer of the University of Sierra Leone focused his praise on Echewa's "remarkably lucid prose style" but quite inexplicably identified the Alsatian missionary to the Igbo as the "hero" of this novel.[3] Inexplicably, however, specialists in African literature have apparently ignored this briefly lauded book completely, despite the publication of subsequent fictional works by Echewa, all of which have also been favourably reviewed on both sides of the Atlantic.

In the present article it is my purpose to take initial steps towards redressing that neglect by focusing on Echewa's pivotal theme of the challenging and ultimately disastrous confrontation of a former contemplative Roman Catholic missionary priest, Father Anton Higler, with Igbo religion and the turbulent natural environment in which it is practised. Of particular interest in this regard is how both his faith and the doctrinal formulations of it were encapsulated in a European cultural shell which inhibited the effectiveness of his mission. A vital second theme is the question of motivation. Echewa explores at length the priest's intentions for entering the religious life in the first place and, after his lengthy stint as a contemplative, leaving a sheltered monastic environment to accept the challenge of propagating the Gospel in an almost virgin mission field.

The Land's Lord is a highly impressive literary work not merely in terms of its ideational content but no less with regard to Echewa's artistic presentation of his central themes of religious interaction and missionary motivation. I shall therefore also analyze the principal and highly effective technique in his narrative of using interlocking parallel elements between the European protagonist and his main convert, a young Igbo man called Philip who faithfully serves him but is caught in a spiritual and emotional tug-of-war between his new beliefs and those of the tribal culture, a momentous dilemma which eventually drives him to suicide. On the surface these two mutually reflecting characters appear to have little in common beyond their commitment to the Roman Catholic Church and their ability to utter certain Latin ecclesiastical phrases. As the plot unfolds, however, Echewa artfully reveals that Higler and Philip are kindred souls with regard to *inter alia* aspects of their troubled earlier lives, their fears, their perceived need for both physical and spiritual defences against their enemies, and nightmares in which they believe they are being possessed by demonic elements. Spiritually, this European missionary and his African convert thus interact to spiral down along parallel paths, victims of the disharmonious relationship between indigenous spirituality and an alien religion which is never really adapted to the Igbo mentality and folkways.

Writing from a conventional point of view as an omniscient narrator, Echewa develops an uncomplicated plot through 145 pages divided into fourteen chapters. The narrative is chiefly lineal, although retrospective thoughts in the increasingly self-doubting mind of the protagonist, an Alsatian Roman Catholic priest of Society of Missionaries of Africa, or White Fathers, who sails to Nigeria to succeed another White Father at Saint Peter Claver mission in a remote and largely unchristian Igbo region near the provincial capital of Aba and the Imo River, reveal much about how poorly he is prepared, both psychologically and missiologically, for this demanding vocation. Precisely when the plot unfolds, Echewa does not state explicitly, although disjointed chronological facts using the First World War as a point of departure suggest approximately two decades after its conclusion, and the fact that Christmas falls on Thursday in the plot indicates that 1940 is the year when he stepped ashore in Africa some fourteen months earlier. Higler is ethnically and culturally isolated there, the only European in a large area. Despite the presence of a considerable number of Igbo villagers, some of whom are members of his parish, "he had no one here," (26) as Echewa writes succinctly. Spiritually, Higler also feels alone, as his nascent parish comprises largely an indeterminate but evidently small number of inverts who by no means have shed the trappings of their animistic tribal religion in favour of monotheism, and a less syncretistic, devoted believer named Philip, who dutifully and without remuneration serves as Higler's domestic servant and liturgical assistant. Culture shock has even driven a wedge between this European-rooted divine and what seems to have become a *Deus absconditus* or *Deus remotus*, at least in a geographical sense. Higler feels early on that "God . . . remained elsewhere far away—as far away it seemed as Europe, where he was held prisoner in the cathedrals." (26) The newly arrived priest dreams of ushering large numbers of Africans into the church, and to accommodate them he begins to erect a spacious chapel which, however, he never completes, owing to the fact that his poverty-ridden congregation must pay for its incremental construction brick-by-brick.

In addition to the struggle inside Higler's head, much of the plot arises from the clash between the emphatically European form of the Christian faith which he proclaims and the deeply ingrained beliefs and practices of the Igbos. Some of the latter willingly accommodate foreign deities, among which they number the God of Christianity, while other villagers are decidedly less latitudinarian. Caught in a spiritual tug-of-war between pressures from his extended family to execute his duties to their clan's gods and his hope of deriving worldly benefits from his new faith, the laconic Philip increasingly evinces symptoms of despair and, ultimately, suicidal depression. Eventually he feels that both his indigenous religion and Christianity have failed him, notwithstanding his years of faithful, unpaid service to the mission. He takes revenge by destroying the interior of Higler's chapel and violating one of the pivotal Igbo taboos by committing incest with a mentally handicapped foster daughter. Meanwhile, Higler's own faith is challenged in pointed conversations with Ahamba, a tribal elder who tolerates the mission but emphatically refuses to convert to Christianity, and shows clear signs of having partly succumbed to despair. During a nocturnal meeting of tribal elders who try Philip for incest, Philip disembowels himself with a machete and Higler, who has attended the tribunal, flees, only to be fished out of a nearby river by Ahamba and a group of Igbo fishermen. *The Land's Lord* ends on an existential note when Ahamba suggests that Philip had fallen victim to his encounter with the truth, i.e. that no deities, tribal or Christian, are capable of satisfying all human needs.

Echewa gradually reveals the Higler, despite his seemingly robust faith and confident personality, is spiritually weak and increasingly questions the authenticity of his call to the mission field. He has known from the outset that he entered the religious life on false pretences. Echewa describes in the fourth chapter how Higler, an erstwhile grocer, had deserted the French army during the battle of Verdun in 1916 and fled to safety across the English Channel. Three weeks later, regarding himself as a "fraud," (32) he had bought a second-hand suit, walked into Saint Mary's Seminary, and announced to one of its leaders, Father Morris, his desire to be admitted to that institution. The suspicious English priest had grilled him about his background and intentions and appeared to realize that Higler had left the army under questionable circumstances, not least when Higler informed him that his vocation had occurred three weeks previously, i.e. at the time of his leaving military service, but nevertheless admitted him, though on the condition that he first serve as a gardener for a year, ostensibly to prove the legitimacy of his vocation. Not until the close of the ninth chapter do readers learn more details of the desertion, including Higler's crucial vow to God, made under heavy shelling, that he would become a priest if he emerged from the battle alive. (98) Few details of Higler's subsequent education and fifteen years as a contemplative in England are given. In any case, his guilt for abandoning his comrades-in-arms apparently had continued to gnaw at him, and he had doubted that God had forgiven him. Seeking assurance, he had longed for an unmistakable sign of divine forgiveness and justification. Apparently this longing remained unfulfilled in England.

Echewa handles Higler's monastic life in Britain summarily and suggests obliquely that little in it was relevant to his short-lived ministry to the Igbos, whose collective mind is incalculably more down-to-earth than that which has shaped his intellect and spirituality. A year after arriving among them, he recalls that "in some fifteen years as a contemplative he had served an abstract God, sublimate and rarified beyond all understanding, had pursued him zealously with a pious faith and in enthusiastic imagination. . . . The twilight of claustrophobic chapels, panelled in heavy oak and haunted by saintly ghosts. Faith supported on a cloud of prayers." (6-7)

The mission field, by contrast, seems to offer the possibility of finally winning assurance of salvation and divine favour. Yet both the chronological rhythms to which Higler has become accustomed as a European contemplative and the neatness of the monastic garden he has faithfully tended in England have left him ill-prepared for the Igbos' seemingly irrational sense of time or the chaotic forest in which they dwell.

Early on Higler learns that his consistently regulated chronology is not that of Africa. "Life here was sometimes painfully slow. At other times it was giddy and spasmodic," (7) he thinks as he takes his daily bath. Higler, who owns the only watch in the area, subsequently perceives that in contrast to his experience in Europe "time in this environment showed reluctance to be divided" other than by the rhythms of nature—the rising and setting of the sun, the phases of the moon, and the rainy and dry seasons. His analytical mind consequently reasons that "life here was not linear, but cyclic and repetitious. Everyone was hitched to a big horizontal circle, and going round and round." (70-71) Rather than adapting, however, Higler seeks to transplant part of his monastic heritage to Igboland in the form of a church bell. Its arrival is nothing less than "the highest point so far in his ministry here" and elevates Higler to a "garrulous and cheerful" mood as he and several young men from the village arduously transport it from a shipping agency in the provincial capital of Aba to Saint Peter Claver mission. (116) Yet even this bell itself underscores the cultural gap between Higler and the Igbo villagers. When the latter eagerly take its rope, "it swung wildly this way and that, whipping its head from side to side like a drunken beast and issuing its call into the wild for miles and miles around." Higler's own use of the device, however, which serves as an expression of his nostalgia, is much more regular, in accord with his monastic experience. The steady pealing of the bell gives him an ally and companion European voice in the jungle. (116-17)

Echewa spills much ink in stressing that the exotic landscape of Igboland not merely poses a pragmatic challenge to Higler but directly threatens the felling of well-being which has been nurtured in him through years of living in an almost idyllic monastic setting. Upon arriving in Igboland, this neophyte missionary realizes immediately that the land provides an environment much different from that to which he has become accustomed in Alsace and England. In the West African forest the Gospel cannot be expected to flourish in the same way as in those European places:

> So this was the Africa he had dreamed about in the last few years, and had sought in his wildest imaginings to re-create mentally in the tame, hallowed and cloistered environs of Saint Mary's, surrounded by an imperially dignified and civilized English countryside, which countryside in comparison to Saint Mary's was considered a defiled 'outside world,' kept at bay by high fences and wrought iron gates and invisible ramparts of divine grace. Even the air on Saint Mary's grounds seemed to be enriched by God's special beneficence, purified and blessed—an island of holiness and tranquillity. During the spring the flowers and the shrubs grew as if they received from God more than the usual compliments of showers and sunshine. Blossoms were large, inflorescences spectacular. To come, to leap from those grounds to this pagan place where the very trees looked sinister and bedevilled! It was like getting a swimming lesson in a sterilized swimming pool and then being cast into a mire pit. There was no protection here, no wall of fence or outer defence perimeter. The jungle and the

> darkness and all that they represented stood close at hand, in front of one's door. (49)

Throughout *The Land's Lord*, Echewa returns to this *leitmotiv* to underscore the role of the physical environment, which its Igbo inhabitants insist with increasing cogency is rife with demonic forces, in challenging and eventually destroying Higler's missionary endeavour.

Perhaps to counter the overwhelming image of unbridled growth in the jungle, which Higler identifies with the threat of demonic powers (an impression fortified by deeply entrenched local religious belief and practices), he meticulously tends a garden at his mission. In his manicured *hortus*, reminiscent of the institution in England where he spent his years as a contemplative, the erstwhile gardener creates at least a miniature plot of what he perceives as metaphoric Christendom, a swatch of manageable soil where he can stave off the forces of Igbo spirits which, he gradually comes to believe, permeate nature in Igboland. "He pulled the weeds off with more than a gardener's zeal, for he saw them not just as vagrant plant growth but as agents of the evil land bent on making his life difficult and his labours fruitless." (105)

Echewa does not contend that Higler lacks essential missionary fervour. Indeed, this priest is grieved by his inability to shepherd large numbers of Igbos into his parish. What gradually emerges from the narrative, however, is a lucid presentation of Higler's interwoven personal motives for sailing to Nigeria. This becomes particularly clear in the priest's perception of the frustratingly slow construction of the gradiose edifice he has planned for the village in which he evangelizes. "If he had not wanted such a big church! But he wanted—needed—a church which was worthy of God and the task that had to be done here, a church that would impress itself on the large skies and endless forests, as well as the pagan villagers." (99-100) In the final chapter the intensely introspective Higler considers his failure as a missionary and of his "illusory hope" of experiencing divine grace through that endeavour. "Cowardice in battle, fear in the face of imminent death, could they by any alchemic trick be turned into virtue, and could an apostleship arising therefore ever attain ennoblement?" (139-40) he asks without the prospect of an affirmative answer from any source. Moments later he flees from physical danger, as he had done at Verdun. Fear thus chronologically brackets Higler's ministry and his search for evidence of God's working in his life.

Echewa also portrays Philip, the pivotal convert and Higler's liturgical and domestic assistant, as a man whose motives for being at the mission are an amalgam of religious fervour and flight from peril. Again, this revelation comes gradually. Initially Philip is a taciturn but obedient churchman, a man of apparent faith who performs his duties without complaint or reservation. In the second chapter Echewa reveals that this convert "had defected from his upbringing, defaulted on his duties as Njoku—acolyte of the farm god," (21) but this is presented merely as factual background without elaboration on its relevance to Philip's earlier or subsequent personal spiritual crises.

In the tenth chapter, Ahamba reveals to Higler that Philip had not merely been attracted to Christianity but had a personal history whose religious aspects echoed a discomfitting episode in the missionary's own past. Referring to Philip as a "coward," the aged Igbo informs Higler that "he ran away from his initiation! Three nights he was to stay in the bush by himself. That is custom. But he ran the first night, which is something that has happened before. Many men have not the heart to face what happens in these bushes you see all around in the middle of the night. . . . He ran and stayed with the other one who came before you and so became pot boiler instead of Njoku." (103)

Various other parallels underscore how Higler's and Philip's spiritual crises mirror one another, despite the waves which their cultural differences give the glass. One of the most clearly symbolic is their mutual desire to possess both religious and secular physical means of defending themselves against their enemies, both objective and imaginary. After feeling overwhelmed by the exotic environment of the forest in which his mission station is located, Higler suffers nightmares and wakes up quivering and feeling utterly vulnerable: "He picked up his rosary from the bedpost and squeezed it, wished he had a gun. Then perhaps he could feel himself as a source of power—some power was better than no power at all—against the amorphous, the generalized and the impalpably palpable dangers that threatened him." (29) Philip's choice of weapons reflects not only a disharmonious marriage of the secular and the profane but also his position straddling his own Igbo culture and the Roman Catholicism which has been bestowed on him in European dress. Clearly shaken by threats made against him by fellow villagers and thus fearing for his life, Philip accepts Higler's invitation to sleep at the station every night instead of returning to his quarters after completing his duties. One night the priest discovers him lying under the altar, clutching a rosary in one hand and a machete in the other. (119) On another occasion Higler finds Philip's own room inexplicably deserted and virtually barren apart from the rosary, the machete, and a bottle of holy water, "a representative coat of arms for Philip in his recent state." (123) These bizarre images serve not merely as signs of the young convert's declining mental stability but also as powerful metaphors for the unholy alliance of forces which encumber the work of the mission.

Other aspects of the Higler's and Philip's background and familial status form appoximate parallels. Higler is a *celibitaire* yet a "father" in a religious sense. Philip has been married but became a widower when his spouse died in childbirth. Higler regards the villagers as spiritually and emotionally his children and believes that intellectually they are decidedly inferior to himself: Philip is not known to have sired any living offspring, yet he must play the role of a parent to his mentally handicapped foster daughter. Higler thinks frequently about his girlfriend Clare whose affection he enjoyed before entering the religious life. She comes to mind at inopportune times, triggering impious thoughts in this lonely priest. An hour before celebrating Christmas Mass, for instance, Higler remembers "the walks in the woods in the late spring. Illicit privileges. Unlicensed and damnable actions. Straddling flesh and spirit, shutting between the dictates of nature and those of nature's God. The celebration of life. Fear. The promises of the imagination and the disappointments of the flesh." (69) One gains the impression that both men are lonely and seek solace and gratification in their religious lives.

Echewa extends the parallelism beyond the two figures to aspects of their birthright religions. Some of these, to be sure, are actually more contrastive than identical. Soon after arriving in Igboland, for example, Higler stumbles across an indigenous altar on which a dog has been sacrificed. The canine carcass is trussed on a wooden structure fashioned from the branches of a tree. Completing the image, "various other objects lay around the altar-egg shells, manilas and cowries, [and] two decorated gourds that might have held some food earlier." (4) The analogy to an amalgam of Catholic sacramental theology and a crucifix on an altar is unmistakable.

The most dynamic of the explicitly religious parallels involves the confusion of spiritual power and its symbolic representations. After arguing with Higler about the necessity of completely giving up what the priest regards as the practice of sacrificing to tribal gods, Philip insists that the *jujus* which depict the latter represent a spiritual reality no less than Christian symbols do. "But Fada," he pleads, "their power is like this cross which I am wearing. It does not come from what it is made of, but what it is." (90) Higler predictably disagrees.

Perhaps both owing to and in spite of their perceived and hidden similarities, Higler and Philip get on well with each other during most of the time which the plot spans. A mutual dependency, after all, links their two lives. Higler needs his convert both as an element of continuity in his nascent church and as an assistant; Philip finds in this priest and his religion a safe spiritual and physical heaven which offers shelter from the wrath of both snubbed *jujus* and resentful relatives. No less vital to the plot of *The Land's Lord*, however, is how both men begin to lose their spiritual stability and unravel emotionally as each comprehends weakness in the anchoring of the other's spirituality. The fact that Higler initially evinces a high degree of confidence without revealing any chinks in his personal armour is particularly essential in this regard.

The crucial scene takes place in the eleventh chapter. Perceiving Philip's fear of his tribal fellows and consequent spiritual plight, Higler seeks to minister to him empathetically by announcing that he is aware that Philip had deserted his initiation duties and explains that he can understand the crisis this has created in the young convert because he, too, has experienced dread. "I ran away from the war," he explains. "Would you believe that? I was in the middle of it and I ran away. That is how I came to be a priest. I deserted under fire. Out of fear . . . I ran, just as you did from your initiation." (111) The amazed Philip cannot believe initially that his Christian spiritual mentor was once afraid. Seeking some *nostrum* for the affliction from which they both had suffered, Philip asks, "What cure did Fada find for his despair?" After approximately two years among the Igbos, however, Higler still has not comprehended their need for physically manifest solutions to their problems and replies with an abstraction which has little chance of being comprehended or satisfying Philip's need: "Hope. One finds a new hope. I found a new hope in the priesthood, in serving God exclusively." His Igbo convert seems willing to listen sympathetically to this seemingly amorphous answer but is nevertheless skeptical and asks whether "Fada's heart is now in complex peace?" Higler further erodes the remnant of Philip's trust and confidence by acknowledging that his spiritual longings remain unrequited. (111) With the key member of his miniscule parish standing before him, the distressed priest ponders the matter silently for a moment before driving the final nail into the coffin of Philip's search for spiritual and emotional satisfaction. "No, Philip. Peace is only a promise. We have been told there can be no peace on this side of heaven. So it is futile to expect it." (112) Visibly shaken, Philip believes that his quest has reached a *cul-de-sac*. "Fada had no answers, only distant hope and promises," he thinks, "His God was like other gods, like the idols and the jujus. So where now? What other God? What other duties and obligations? What other hopes of freedom held before the slave to keep him slaving harder? The horizon that kept moving back and moving back, no way to reach it, no way to come even close to it." (112) Shortly thereafter, the despairing Philip takes his revenge by destroying the chapel and committing incest. Rather than bringing salvation and palpable manifestations of hope in accordance with the demands of Igbo culture, Higler has merely compounded this convert's despair. *The Land's Lord* contains elements of classic tragedy, and Higler's tragedy thus becomes Philip's tragedy.

Echewa's debut novel is not a frontal assault on Christianity as such, and he does not lay the blame for the cultural turbulence of colonial Nigeria at the doorsteps of Christian missionaries who propagated their faith in that country. *The Land's Lord* is arguably more profitably read as a blistering critique of the inadequate preparation, questionable motivation, and condescending attitudes of those missionaries whom the highly realistic if unrepresentative character of Father Anton Higler represents. Furthermore, this book is a work of fiction which embodies a high degree of artistic competence, but it is not an historical novel to which scholars of the proliferation of Roman Catholicism in Nigeria would profitably turn in search of a reliable first-hand account of the advent of the church among the Igbos. Read naively, *The Land's Lord* leaves the impression that during the early 1940s Christianity was virtually unknown in Igboland, when in fact it had become quite firmly entrenched in the part of Nigeria by the outbreak of the First World War. The interdenominational front included a significant Catholic dimension. As early as 1913 the Irish Holy Ghost priest Joseph Shanahan could write that "at last the era of Patrick is being realised in Igboland. As we move from town to town, idols are toppling of their own accord and the Cross of Christ is being erected in their place."[4] His optimism was argubaly misleading, yet by 1918 the area reportedly numbered 13042 baptised Roman Catholics, 37929 catechumens, and 22838 scholars.[5] There were no fewer than 355 Catholic schools and churches at that time, most of them undoubtedly quite small. The organisations which had undertaken and maintained evangelistic work in Nigeria did not at that time include the White Fathers, or Society of Missionaries of Africa, founded in Algeria in 1868, which did not accept a mission there until after the Second World War.[6]

The Land's Lord nevertheless rings true with regard to most of the central issues with which Echewa deals. His highlighting of Higler's cultural captivity and the devastating results of his concomitant failure to adapt his Christian message to Igbo culture echoes a refrain heard on many mission fields for centuries. Echewa's description of tensions between Christian Igbos and their non-Christian neighbours also has a high degree of verisimilitude. Writing a year before the publication of *The Land's Lord*, Emmanuel Obiechina of the University of Nigeria faulted Igbo converts to Christianity for failing to appeal to "clan solidarity" and being "obsessed with their own importance and contemptuous of all non-initiates." He lamented the tendency of this Christian faction to create unnecessary social cleavages by referring condescendingly to the adherents of African traditional religions in their minds as "the people of nothing."[7] In 1960 Chinua Achebe, himself an eagle-eyed observer of Igbo culture and the impact of Christianity on it, expressed it less acerbically in his acclaimed novel *No Longer at Ease*; his Christians call the others "the people of the world."[8] This, too, *mutatis mutandis*, has been a recurrent theme in much of Christendom, not least in many mission fields. Although the plot of *The Land's Lord* unfolds in a remote corner of Igboland, involves only one Christian denomination, and spans less than two years, it thus addresses masterfully themes of relevance on a much wider cultural, denominational, and chronological scale.

NOTES

1. Charles R. Larson, "Anglophone Writing from Africa and Asia," *World Literature Today*, LI, no. 2 (Spring 1977), p. 235.
2. Kolawole Ogungbesan, "West Africa," *The Journal of Commonwealth Literature*, XII, no. 3 (April 1978), p. 37.
3. Eustace Palmer, "T. Obinkaram Echewa: *The Land's Lord*," *International Fiction Review*, IV, no. 2 (July 1977), pp. 167-68.
4. John P. Jordan, *Bishop Shanahan of Southern Nigeria* (Dublin: Clonmore & Reynolds, 1949), p. 109.
5. Adrian Hastings, *The Church in Africa 1450-1950* (Oxford: Clarendon Press, 1994), p. 450.
6. For the history of the Society of Missionaries of Africa, see Glenn D. Kittler, *The White Fathers* (London: W.H. Allen, 1957) and Elizabeth Mary Matheson, *African Apostles* (New York: Alba House, 1963).
7. Emmanuel Obiechina, *Culture, Tradition and Society in the West African Novel* (Cambridge: Cambridge University Press, 1975), p. 219.
8. Chinua Achebe, *No Longer at Ease* (London: Heinemann, 1960), p. 58.

Satire and Comedy in the Novels of T.M. Aluko

R.M.V. RAGHAVENDRA RAO

In his critique of the works by the post-independence generation of West Africa, Claude Wauthier states that they do more than express their disillusionment with their native society and government: "they often constitute a violent indictment of the political depravity that has become the norm in many countries, this indictment which often takes the form of bitter satire, is all the more striking in view of the fact that the number of writers who choose to deal with the themes of corruption, nepotism and the incompetence of the African politicians in power seems to increase!"[1]

Nigeria, torn by internal quarrels and a series of coups culminating in the secession of Biafra has given rise to new breed of novels with the bitterest indictments. The feeling of utter dissatisfaction with Nigerian political life found its first expression in Cyprian Ekwensi's *Jagua Nana*, in 1961. If Soyinka and Okara can be cited as novelists with emphasis on satire as social criticism, Achebe's ambivalent attitude towards Igbo culture "plainly points to a disposition of mind which is likely to lead to the creation of satirical fiction.[2]

Viewed against this situation of the modern Nigerian novel, Aluko strikes the reader as being purely satirical from the first to the last of his five novels.[3] In all these, Aluko reacts sharply to a society weakened by greed and intolerance, poverty, ignorance, disease, religion and struggle for power—themes insightfully treated by him.

The little critical attention Aluko has received so far itself may speak as much for the departures made by Aluko from the fictional tradition of the Nigerian novel as social criticism, as for the lack of sophisticated craft in his novels. Aluko's novels are overtly satirical in their bitter criticism of the uncritical acceptance of the indigenous traditions, beliefs and superstitions by the people in the face of the challenges of modern experience. His novels dramatize the predicament of the native culture at the point of history when it confronted the Western interference in its day-to-day life and political administration. They expose the Nigerian ways unsparingly—the opportunism, the fears and the ambivalence against the white man's assaults on them. But, in the only known exhaustive attempt to study Aluko as a novelist, Bernth Lindfors underrates Aluko's position as a satirist and considers him "a light-hearted comedian."[4]

The present paper attempts to identify the redeeming qualities of satire in Aluko's novels—wit, irony, parody, the comic force, the African vernacular style and above all an overall moral vision, free from gloom, though bordering on fun.

Aluko's first novel, *One Man One Wife* deals with polygamy and church politics in a newly Christianized society. Joshua, the main character, is distressed when he learns that the new religion forbids him to marry a second wife, for he has already paid his bride-price on a preadolescent girl named Toro. Joshua tries to marry off Toro to his son Jacob who refuses her and marries Joke. Four days after the marriage, Joke proves to be pregnant by another man. Joshua and Joke die and the interest of the novel shifts to Royanson, an expelled church member who styles himself as "Public Letter Writer and Notary, Friend of the Illiterate, Advocate of the Oppressed." Eventually he goes mad and Jacob and Toro are brought back to finish out the story. The last part of the novel describes a small-pox epidemic, a court case, a suicide, and a sudden religious conversion.

The meandering plot of the novel is redeemed by wit and satire. Aluko pokes fun at the old order as well as the new. The conflict between the two is replete with humour. At the betrothal ceremony of Joshua with Toro, Bada points out that Christianity is a great menace in the village and an affront to the mighty Shonponna, the God of small-pox, worshipped by Isolo people. The small-pox itself is considered to have come from the White Man's country, and that it was his religion.

> In that case the villagers could not drive away the village Christians without exposing themselves to the anger of the White Man. "These are serious words. Elders of Isolo, what shall we do?" The Asolo of Isolo again asked, worried. No one answered. One of them, the old chief Lotun, snored softly. (97-98)

Such serious analysis and arguments end up only in the people's inaction and slumber, like the responses of the Elders of Isolo and chief Lotun.

One Man One Wife is also an expression of Aluko's direct attack on the discipline imposed on headstrong girls who violate marriage contracts.

> A daughter who refused to marry the suitor of her parent's choosing was invariably sent to the OBA's palace. . . . A new member of the large harem, she would be attached as a ward to an elderly wife for whom she would slave as a domestic servant while she learnt in return the endless tradition writes and the many Don'ts that went with the life in the palace. The new bride was one of scores . . . indeed, most of them were the mistresses of his [Oba's] elder son's relatives and hangers-on. (108-9)

Satire against tradition is too direct in Aluko and provides a glaring foil to Achebe's objectivity, though a preoccupation with the past is shared by the novels of both. In this connection, Arthur Drayton states, Aluko "has attempted to do for Yoruba land what [Achebe] has done for Ibo land, namely, to present an image of the past at that point where the civilization of the western world came into contact with it. . . . [Aluko's] is almost a total rejection of the past."[5]

Aluko's next novel, *One Man One Matchet* has sharper satirical thrusts centred around the activities of Benjamin, an ill-educated politician and journalist. He instigates people against a new African District Officer, Udo Akpan, and opposes cutting down diseased cocoa trees. His opportunism and exploitation ends in his death in the hands of one of his own followers. The novel presents the culture conflict effectively in the character of Udo who fights the corrupt society. While the unscrupulous Benjamin is exposed through his own pompous and hypocritical utterances to the gullible people, even Udo is a target of satire due to his own self-contradictory ways. He has an African way of assessing problems but behaves like an expatriate officer. Hence the appellation "the black White man." His odd conviction is that the people can accept the colonization by making the system work effectively.

Kinsman and Foreman, Aluko's third novel, is a perfect blend of satire and comedy at its best. It has the familiar theme in African fiction of a native returning after western education to find himself at odds with his native culture, backward due to its unshakeable superstitions, the corrupt officers and the people's gullibility. Titus Oti earns from London as the first professionally qualified Nigerian civil engineer posted as District engineer at Ibale. On the death of Oti's father during Oti's stay in London, Simeon Oke the foreman in the P.W.D. is made Oti's kinsman, due to a family connection between them. Oti's integrity and Simeon's corruption provide a dramatic tension not only in terms of individual character but also between the rational and critical perspectives of an evolved individual wanting change and reform and a society resisting change.

Oti's confrontation with the society starts with a letter from the Harvest Committee of All Souls Church inviting him to be the chief opener at the Bazaar Sale that year which honour implies a heavy donation from him to the Committee. Oti's integrity prevents him from such an involvement.

Simeon's brazen dishonesty as foreman, Oti's disapproval of it, the legal battle and the judgement acquitting Simeon forms the core of the novel, the irony striking the reader in the popular support that Simeon enjoys during his prosecution and the people's distress at the possibility of his dismissal.

Oti cannot accommodate the idea of so many father-figures and the loyalty to the members of the extended family. He reacts to the contradictions in human character by expressing himself candidly to Bola, his fiancee abroad. Writing about Pa Joel's evidence in Simeon's prosecution, he writes.

> I was tempted to ask her [Oti's mother] if she knew that Pa Joel's evidence was influenced by his great fear of Olude the family God to speak the truth as to whether or not he had given the piece of land to Simeon . . . his Christianity is only skin-deep. He believes more in his Olude who he thinks can cause him a violent death than in the God he goes to worship at the church twice every Sunday. Pastor now named Marakinyo's fault, to my mind. He has painted the Christian God as a forgiving father, slow to chide and swift to bless. (171)

The ironic tone of Oti is very prominent towards the end of the novel which builds up a hilarious climax in the euphoria following the claim of the tribal head Bandele that he had visions "to the effect that the end of the world was truly coming," (172) the Judgement Day falling on 12th August. Urging Bola in all transparent light-heartedness to come back and get married to him, he writes: Have you thought of all this? Nonsense, of course. But remember that it is written in the Scriptures that Last Day will come and catch people completely unprepared.

So, my girl, you had better give more thought to your religious exercises than your own devotion may save both you and sinful me from the wrath to come." (172)

Again, as narrator, Aluko speaks out the mind of Oti on various occasions. When the Judgement Day does not come through and Iþala and the community of Alasoteles shoots into world news becoming the food of reporters, Oti thought, "the men of Isala would have got over their disappointment at not being sucked into the Biblical paradise on 12 August 1950, and gone back to their farms . . . if they had been left alone. The little town has been invaded by newspaper reporters" (198) or again, as Oti recalls the thesis in an article, he reflects, "It has been obvious for sometime to scholars of theology and of contemporary Christianity, that the Second Coming of the Lord would be through a village in black Africa. This was to demonstrate God's disapproval of racial discrimination." (199)

The novel ends on the assertion of the lawyer Chris that Simeon got acquitted despite all his confessions on the supposed day of Judgement and despite all the facts against him, because of "the very elementary fact that neither the house of Elder Matthew nor its precincts had been properly constituted into a court of law." (202)

Kinsman and Foreman is also distinct from the earlier novels for the bits of dialogue in African vernacular style such as those in the introduction of Oti to Simeon in the opening pages of the novel which shows the potential of a vernacular register. According to Lindfors, in *Kinsman and Foreman* "Aluko has come a long way in a short time." (48)

Chief the Honourable Minister recounts the rise of a school teacher, Alade Moses, from Member of Parliament to Minister. But he remains a resigned observer of corruption in the Government and the intrigues of the foreign embassies. A bloody battle between the armed men of the Government supporters and those of the opposition is the outcome of a rigged election. The book ends with the army seizing power. One passage in which the Prime Minister showers sarcastic praise on Moses reads as follows:

> A great English scholar once observed that when we see genius come out of what looks like the gutter we should know that it did not begin there. If we take the trouble to dig beneath the surface we will discover that like Shakespeare the son of a wood-pedlar, Napoleon the son of a farmer, and Luther the son of a peasant, the genius from the guttermost probably descended from a line of

> kings and prophets. That observation was made about one of the greatest figures of history, Abraham Lincoln. It may well be applied here and now to your own son Alade Moses. (176)

The far-fetched comparisons and illusions, by their inappropriateness only project the satirical intention of the author. The novel is a pungent satire on personalities and ideas of the government. Aluko expresses his bitterness towards an incorrigible political situation through the reports of a newspaper, *Sentinel*, in passages such as the follows:

> The wrath of the God of Africa will descend upon them, the perpetrators of this monstrous crime against the electorate of the nation. And Nemesis will come to all the organs and institutions of society that have aided and abetted the crime. All of them that have made a complete mockery of the sacred institution of the ballot box, all of them that stood in the way of the people's exercising their inalienable right to choose who shall speak for them in the nation's assembly—all of them will pay the penalty at the appointed time. (32)

The passage is full of exaggerations, repetitions and rhetoric. Moses ends up in a ridiculous situation of doubts and mental agony and the target of the Prime Minister's ironic praise. The novel, according to Oladele Taiwo, "reveals Aluko's sardonic intent." (91)

His Worshipful Majesty, Aluko's fifth novel, deals with the authority of the king in Nigeria in conflict with the local Government law meant for modernisation. Alaiye, king of Aiye, commands unquestioned authority over his small kingdom. But since the British have come to hold some reins of power and the form the Divisional Council for development of education, hospitals and roads, the king's power stands questioned. He is made to realize that he has become accountable for the public money and that his time-honoured ways cannot continue.

Narrated by Kale Roberts, the Secretary in the Aiye local authority, the novel elaborately presents the ritualistic pomp of various ceremonies and complexities of tradition. In the 5th and 6th chapters, the sacrifice of the goats and songs in praise of Gods, Osin and Ela, and the king are vividly brought out. Even as the Council questions the king's authority to use the public resources for his Royal comfort and even as its members question the propriety of raising the king's salary, they fail to face the king when confronted with the king's ire. In one such incident,

Eketa, a chief, pleads for the king's mercy by going down on his tummy. "The chief rolled from side to side on the bare concrete floor" or "the unfortunate old man licked the dusty concrete floor." (61) Apart from the fright of the Royal authority, the king's supposed divinity inflicts a severe punishment of the chief. "The Eketa was stricken with paralysis of right arm and the right leg two days later." (62)

Even in this mixed situation of tradition trying to hold on to itself at any cost, and the experiments of modernization, there are the corrupt who make good of the volatile situation. In one of the council meetings, the Treasurer tells the Chairman that the chiefs have never been paid any salaries. When the Chairman asks in all seriousness, "just how do they live," the reaction of the people is as follows:

> Most people laughed, most people knew what he did not know, that both the salaried and the non-salaried chiefs lived mainly on taxes, both taxes collected and taxes not collected. Each chief was responsible for the collection of taxes in his area . . . the tax evader paid a bribe of a quarter or a third of the flat rate assessment, and the chief was that much richer through a single client. If both sides were happy, why should anyone worry. (64)

Through Kale's apparently candid but sarcastic reportage, the novel records the turbulent events in a state of dual administration, of the king and the council at loggerheads. The appeal lies in the blend of the serious and the funny such as the account of the community revenge of the monkeys or gifts offered to the king by the people such as the carcass of a lion with the faith that it is a lion for a lion. The corruption itself is reported in a matter-of-factness, oversimplifying its effect as a crime. Roberts states: "I have heard that the white man who does not understand our customs considers this as bribery and corruption, but I have always known that expressing gratitude by means of a gift is part and parcel of our way of life." (90)

In the episode on the Commission of inquiry into the royal household the novelist not only exposes the superfluity and absurdity of the king's establishment but also the white man's ignorance of the traditional establishment that goes with the royalty of the king. When the Commissioner does not understand the duties of a particular horse man, the counsel for the royal household explains to him, "this witness here is in charge of assisting royalty up and down a particular horse which has been selected for the particular occasion." (119) A funnier witness is that of Bada, chief of the palace boys. When questioned about his duties, much to the astonishment of the Commissioner, he states, "my duty is to die with king." (120) What follows is a further inquiry into the frequency at which this duty is performed.

The earlier novel, *Chief the Honourable Minister*, records the account of the emergence of a military government, earned by the people whose ruling leaders and the controls on them are equally corrupt and the degeneration of the only hope, that is the teacher who has become a minister. In *His Worshipful Majesty,* Aluko goes back to the institution of the king and the onset of the British Imperial rule and the pathetic and futile efforts of the king to retain the reins of power, even as they are weakened and defeated, ironically by a fanatical adherence to the ineffective tradition. The king in this novel is ruined by his own ignorance and blind faith in the White man's rule. King Alaiye only wants the replacement of one Governor or Resident with another from the Crown till his own "dirge" is sung. Clinging on to the memory of the historic moment when the great Treaty of Friendship and Commerce was made between the Queen of Great Britain, Ireland and Empress of India and the king and chiefs of Aiye, he becomes a part of history as he wants Roberts "to write the truth about us in your book." (175)

This novel is an indictment on tradition, and its incapacity to be strong in the face of change as much as a bitter exposure of the surreptitious ways of the White man to replace it culturally and temporally.

Nevertheless, to consider Aluko a satirist without the anguish and vision of Achebe or Soyinka is to ignore the subtlety of his empathy for the Nigerian cultural and political situation caught forever, as it were, in the throes of instability.

Soyinka told a gathering of African writers in 1967, "The time has come when the African writer must have the courage to determine what alone can be salvaged from the recurrent cycle of human stupidity."[6] In the same context he also insisted on a "very definite vision" on the part of the writer: "He must at least begin by exposing the future in a clear and truthful exposition of the present." (58)

Aluko's satirical fiction may not have a definite vision of the future as yet, but certainly has a commitment to the exposition of the African past. Aluko's novels present a constant dialogue between tradition and the challenge of change with deceptive casualness and bitterness betraying a concern for the condition of his society. If they are light-hearted, certainly they are not self-indulgent or sardonic. They expose the truth in blows, subtly delivered.

NOTES

1. Claude Wauthier, *The Literature and Thought of Modern Africa* (London: Heinemann, 1978), p. 318.
2. Oladele Taiwo, *Social Experience in African Literature* (Nigeria: Fourth Dimension, 1986), p. 123.
3. T. M. Aluko, *One Man One Wife* (London, 1967); *One Man One Matchet* (London, 1967); *Chief the Honourable Minister* (London, 1970); *His Worshipful Majesty* (London, 1973).
4. Bernth Lindfors, "T.M. Aluko: Nigerian Satirist," *African Literature Today*, No. 5, 1971, p. 53.
5. Arthur Drayton, "The Return to the Past in the Nigerian Novel," *Ibadan*, No. 10 (1960), p. 29 (quoted in Lindfors's article on Aluko, p. 43).
6. Wole Soyinka, "The Writer in a Modern African State," *The Writer in Modern Africa* (Uppasala, Scandinavian Institute of African Studies, 1968), p. 20.

Ben Okri's *Flowers and Shadows* Or The Difficult Happy Medium

ANDRE H. TOLOFON

Ben Okri makes the social sickness inherent in and brought about by the rush for money and power the central theme of his first novel, *Flowers and Shadows*.[1] The description of his characters's inner landscapes and the complexity of the themes evidence the debut of a promising artist. Okri delves into the analysis of his society, which, with the shift from traditional codes of conduct, gives birth to a new breed of psychologically-unbalanced characters.

The novel, the setting of which is an unnamed Nigerian village and Lagos, reveals the loneliness and despair of men and women at grips with the realities of a society no longer acting as one.

In fact *Flowers and Shadows* is the story of a Nigerian modern family: Jonan Okwe, the father, Lizzi, his wife and their only son, Jeffia. They live in Lagos where Jonan is a businessman. Try as he may to provide his family with all necessary life amenities, his household still lacks love and harmony. Jonan is so engrossed in his business that he cannot see that his wife and son are unhappy. One of the reasons for his behaviour can be traced back to the hard life he had as a child: "His childhood had been rough. He had worked endlessly in the farm with his father. In the mornings he had to trek to the only school in the district that was miles away. His whole life seemed to him like that, no sweetness anywhere." (99) To crown it all, a crisis which has taken the form of a plague, sweeping away all those who were without money, bereaved Jonan of his father. The plague and the death of his father tolled the knell of the we-are-all-brothers spirit which had prevailed in the village till then. With his father's maxim-like advice "Poverty is a curse" as the only legacy, Jonan disembarked in Lagos, ready to "master the hard, ruthless, unwritten rules of business in Nigeria at that time." (11)

The hostile social atmosphere he lived in has an obvious bearing on

Jonan's personality. Education being of utmost importance in man's life, its influence which comes from the parents, the environment and the prevalling ideas follows the individual everywhere he goes. The restrictions and segregation based on money as new obstacles in the way to self-achievement in Nigerian society have created a state of psychic disequilibrium in Jonan. The repression of the psychic existential needs through which he could seek the friendship, the love, the company of other men and through which he could be related to the natural world has led to a break, a deficit in his personality, hence to the birth of a pathological superego. He thinks and acts conformably to his father's prescriptions. He becomes a fearful, anxious, stiff character. To compensate for the deficit in him, he overdevelops a self-assertive aggression which results in an inordinate, immoderate ambition. Jonan's sentiment of obsession born from his feeling of humiliation frustrates all his other motives and behaviour.

Flowers and Shadows is built up on the gap existing between the new values and their practical implementation. Jonan's conflict is in his dogged determination to attain his goal and his inability to handle his human relationship. The traumatic experience he underwent in his childhood has left marks on his psyche. According to Freud, the libido, in a normal evolution, goes through the auto-erotic stage to the object-love stage. In Jonan's case, due to his childhood experience, his libido has stopped half-way on the narcissistic phase. "Many people linger unusually long in their condition, and many of its features are carried over by them into the later stages of their development."[2]

Since Jonan thinks his society is the reason for his mishap and slight, he turns his back to everybody, transferring his libido from the external world to his ego. Hence, only his person, his needs, his thoughts and belongings are what matters. Everything outside him or useless to him is not "fully real." His self-cult results from the fact that the libido withdrawn from the outer world "becomes attached to the ego, and used for the aggrandizement of the ego. A return is thus made to the stage of narcissism, in which a person's only sexual object is his own ego."[3] As he feels inferior, scorned at and persecuted, he lapses into egocentricity and delusions of grandeur. He moves heaven and earth to make people forget the disgrace and humiliation brought on his family.

> He remembered his father had died young, consumed by an unfathomable disease, streaks covering his whole body. They had

> burnt his remains. He remembered how his people of the village began to isolate him, how they disposed of his father's property. . . . The most important thing for him became to make something of his life. To make money and be rich. It didn't take him long to realise that only money and power had any real meaning, and only money and power could make him survive without fear of the past. (171)

Jonan's narcissistic inflation urges him to seek success at any cost, since a failure might result in depression or insanity. Goaded on as he is by the passion consuming him, he gets carried away in a deluding world.

> He soon acquired that implicit sense of power and satisfaction of being able to say 'I told you so' to those who always doubted the things he always believed strongly he could do.
>
> But the satisfaction and sense of power reached a stage when they turned into a paranoia, into an obsession, restless and uncompromising to possess and subjugate. (12)

With one eye for detail, Okri brings home to the reader Jonan's self-love through the portrait of himself, hanging in his office and in which, like the Greek hero, he admires his own image as though filling himself with his power and inner strength. His megalomania is emphasized in the description of the luxury and size of his offices: "large as tennis courts, oak-pannelled, sound-proofed walls with filigree designs and rare art pieces hanging on them." (11) His long frustration, his trauma and the ensuing fixation have led him to blindly take up the "harsh ruthless and unwritten rules" laid down by his society. His new world is one which allows the stronger to downtread the weaker with impunity. "The society in which we live is a complex one. To get anything out of it you have to rise above the system. . . . We are in a large entangled web of law and disorder, power, waste and misuse. And in this crazy society it is power people that really count. All the rest are means to an end. My choice was wealth and power. I have had my share of people who passed through my fingers." (74)

As we have said, the education given to a child helps build his superego, "a replica of all the commandments and prohibitions of the father with whom the little boy identifies himself."[4] The above norms are made up by society for its own harmonious functioning, the superego playing the regulating part. In Jonan's society, we wonder whether the superego can fulfill that function, given that a large sector of the individual "psychic structure is the product of adaptation of his class and the whole society in which he lives."[5] Subtly, Ben Okri pinpoints the absence of that moral regulator.

Not only is Jonan's superego conditioned by fatherly norms, it also mirrors the social change taking place in Africa. It reflects the individualistic social patterns, governed by money.

While the will to climb out of poverty can be construed as the first reason for Jonan's behaviour, the attainment of power has infused him with more egotism. His fighting spirit becomes pathological. Success causes in him lack of balance insofar as it does not permit him to look back and throw a critical eye on his doings.

Many hints show that deep inside him, there is room for emotion, love and pity. The cultural stereotype definition of a man in his society does not allow him to show emotion, which is the characteristic of a woman. He then becomes impervious to everything which could divert him from his goal. He has no interest in those who invest themselves in what he calls "petty unrealistic values." Considering the close relationship between his wife and his son Jeffia, he is afraid the latter should turn into a social castrate: "Jonan looked from one to the other with vague contempt., especially Jeffia. He has long concluded Jeffia would grow up soft and lazy like a woman. He was too close to his mother and too soft in his values. What did Jeffia see in flowers. He wondered if the sons of today could be as tough as the sons of yesterday. There is too much book now, too many petty unrealistic values." (137)

Lest Jonan should be looked down on as a failure, he has suppressed everything that could remind him of his father.[6] His society has designed a new system based on rationality and action. A man showing tenderness or emotion is not really manly. Stifling therefore his anima, the feminine qualities in him, has become for Jonan synonymous with "progress and action." That is why he cannot get along with his son and wife. That is why he disapproves of Jeffia's liking for painting, flowers, movies for "they never did a thing for you, never solved one of your problems. It was the same with religion, a thing people did because they were stupid creatures of fancy and fear. They were even more foolish to think that a god was supposed to be out there in the reaches of space care about the problems and sufferings and deaths of people here on earth." (135) As a "very functional man," Jonan's preference goes to things he can touch and enjoy. to people he can use as a spring-board.

He has married Lizzi, a defenceless orphan, to feel he is a strong man, a complete man. His love for his wife and son can be seen as a disguised way to self-love. As he is completely self-centred, he renders useless his living-room that should be a meeting-place for all the family; consequently, not only are all the members of his household physically locked up in their several rooms, but also "they remained locked up in their private worlds." (139)

The fear to be thought weak has biased his judgement. He has become indifferent to other's misfortunes or sufferings. He then discards all the nightmares, fears and presentiments of his wife as "feminine pastime."

> While she reacted by having nightmares and being ill and delicate, he reacted by being more energetic and all-consuming in his business. She was preoccupied with her fears, too disturbed with them. He was too preoccupied with succeeding more and more, that he had no room in his mind for such depressing thoughts. (74)

All his energies are so oriented towards his all-consuming passion, that is typified by his greed for money, power and fame that he forgets about all those who care for him. As a result, his wife becomes sick from trembling for his safety and his son rebels against him. His friends, if there are any, are "those who know what they want from each other." (18)

In the basic conflict between life instincts in man's biological constitution and the death ones, Jonan has not been able to maintain the balance. Consequently, he cannot help directing his drives towards destructiveness, either against himself or against the world around. Nobody is spared. Everybody becomes a pawn on his way up. The society in which he lives is interesting so far as it serves his needs. "In this crazy society it is the power people that really count. All the rest are means to an end." (74)

He leads a near outcast life, contenting himself with mirroring his superiority in the inferiority of his subordinates. He belittles, humiliates his employees and makes them feel they need him. To achieve this end, he resorts to all sorts of means. He crushes all those who happen to stand in his way, all those who thwart his plans. Jeffia's portrayal of him is more telling.

> My father . . . hard as adamant. Sometimes he reminded me of what I had read about Mafia bosses. He had brazened out the likes

> of hurricanes and monsoons . . . he had left broken structures on the roads over which he had passed . . . he had broken fragile stalks of flowers that grew in the fields adjacent to his interests. (182)

Jonan has been so busy framing, spying, dismissing and even killing those who have become useless or a threat to him that he has not realised the cracks in his life edifice. His deep-felt need to live down his past makes him act without circumspection. It has not mattered to him to know that the trade union in his company has been calling for action, that a great many of his skilled workers have resigned and that a new rival paints company has been gaining ground, thus, undermining his. Beside all this, there are his wife's psychological disturbances and his son's rebellious attitude. But all those problems are not enough to curb his passion or demoralize him, not even the heart attack he has had because of overworking and psychological strain. He has his ways of overcoming any plight. For example, looking at his large portrait in which the artist has put "a flattering calm, confident expression on his face . . . would stir some power within him and he would feel an inner strength." (14) He has always managed to get out of the many predicaments he has had in his life, but the one he is facing now seems quite different from all the others. So, however much he looks at his portrait, it arouses nothing. Instead of the impassive self-assertive Jonan he is used to, he sees himself as he is in actual fact: an anxious man, afraid of his past and of his real self. His thoughts in a complete disarray, he turns to rituals and occult forces in order to ward off ill-fortune and have the upper hand over those whom he considers jealous of his success. But the performance of the rites of his juju comes to no avail. To Ben Okri, Jonan's disarray is nothing else than the contradictions in the mind of the modern African who has chosen to turn his back to his past, to everything that leads to oneness in man: religion, nature and other men. The irony in Jonan's situation is that the forces and the man that have helped him climb up are the same that have brought about his downfall.

In fact, Sowho is the one who has had the idea of a paints company. He has taken contact with the mother company, and Jonan "edged himself into the deal," assuring Sowho that what belongs to one belongs to both of them. But to get rid of Sowho, his half-brother, Jonan has framed him for theft. Sowho has subsequently been jailed. Now, he is out of prison and determined to destroy the callous Jonan. His tactics have been simple but effective. He has secretly undermined Jonan's position by first spying on him, then arousing his workers against him and sending anonymous phone calls to blackmail him and choosing the right moment to come out of the shadows for a final confrontation. In the fight that has followed, both get killed. Thus, as Sowho on whom Jonan has climbed to reach up has prophesied, "the wickedness he has done" has bounced back at him. Jonan's mulish determination not to resemble his father has driven him to the same shameful end. His resolution to adhere to the new social patterns as a way out has proved a failure.

By delving into his characters' psychic disturbances, Okri pinpoints the forces at work in the modern African's mind. In the rush for money and the dream of self-aggrandizement, the modern African is leading an incomplete life, because overlooking the essential. He has left himself groomed to forget that man's full development dwells on the development of all vital aspects in him. Jonan has striven to foster his manly qualities only. By doing so, he has rendered his existence superficial. Ridden by the fear of ending up like his deceased father, he fails to see things with his own eyes. Everything is assessed in the light of the precept laid down by his superego.

In a society whose collective code of conduct is based on the law of the jungle, there is no community life. All attempts of the group at creating a powerful and binding whole are doomed to failure because individuals are not driven by the same interests. Only disorder, brutality, aggressiveness and violence as social foundations can be the consequences. The blind rat race for pleasure, honour and power deprives man of true happiness. Seeing the world just from one angle, the individual neglects all the treasures hidden inside him. For Jonan, flowers, nature and works of art have nothing to offer man. Owing to his psychological blocks, he is unable to apprehend what is beyond the visible and the concrete.

Through Jonan's anxieties, quest and tragedy, Ben Okri reveals a world at grips with an unprecedented crisis: that of man. The introduction of individualistic values into the traditional social make-up has led people to repress the values which had been their frames of reference. As a consequence, man is now confronted with a situation of permanent uncertainty.

The core of man's problem is his greed for the above-mentioned values, with no room for emotions and dreams. By combating material poverty at any cost, Jonan has paved the way for another poverty, that of the heart; neglecting what makes a human humane, he has fallen in the trap of aggressiveness and loneliness, which clearly points to "a symptom of psychical dysfunctioning, of inner emptiness and a lack of center within oneself. It is a pathological manifestation of the failure to develop fully."[7]

Ben Okri has shown his talent to the full in his handling of his main character's flaws and the deep motivations behind Jonan's actions. It is needless to say that Jonan's tragedy is symptomatic of a deep social and psychological malaise. From his point of observation, Okri imparts his message to the reader: Man, far from being a fragment in the universe, a separated tiny part of nature, is an "homo symbolicus," that is he is at one with every existing thing. The irony in Jonan's situation is that like grim death, he clings to material possession to attain self-therapy and thus live down his father's failure. His tragedy is the one awaiting our world if the cure for the psychological split left by the invasion of the new values is a rush for the acquisition of the same new values. The last image Okri gives of Jonan and his half-brother is suggestive. "There was a clanging din of crashing metal and the two cars tumbled on their sides. The next moment they burst into flames." The way out as the writer seems to suggest between the lines, lies in the reconciliation of the self with the self, the self with his environment. That is what Jeffia, thanks to Cynthia, his girl friend, has understood.

> Just me and the elements. Then I could be alone with myself and hold child-like conversation with the wind and the open sky. . . . I was in no hurry, I had come to find peace with myself and my memories. I had long ago discovered there was no such thing as finding peace outside oneself in the heat of a life's journey or in the hustle for material acquisition. . . . In the harmony of sounds all around me I thought I could discern echoes of an elusive symphony love flowed out of me. (196-97)

Jonan has never sought to experience such a feeling, being a one-track-minded person. Cut off from himself as from his environment, he is unable to journey back into himself for a self-rediscovery. Okri uses Jonan and his plight to remind us that harmony, love and happiness are not without us, but within. In the end, though Amokoko slums, the refuge of Jonan's family after his death, are dirty and the roads uncared for, Jeffia, Lizzi and Cynthia have discovered there another dimension of happiness and peace.

NOTES

1. Ben Okri, *Flowers and Shadows* (Halow: Longman, 1980).
2. Sigmund Freud, *Case Histories II* (Harmondsworth: Pelican, 1974), Vol. 9, p. 198.
3. *Loc. cit.*
4. Erich Fromm, *The Crisis of Psychoanalysis* (Greenwich, Conn.: Fawcet, 1970), p. 53.
5. *Ibid.*, p. 127.
6. Jonan's difficult start in life reminds one of Okonkwo in Achebe's *Things Fall Apart*. In point of fact, both Jonan's and Okonkwo's fathers died poor.
7. Erich Fromm, *The Anatomy of Destructiveness* (Holt: Rinehart and Winston, 1973), p. 208.

A Study of Nature-Culture Forces in Arun Joshi's *The Strange Case of Billy Biswas* and Ngugi wa Thiong'o's *The River Between*

G.D. BARCHE

From time immemorial man's life has been guided and governed by two eternal forces, viz. Nature-Culture, Swadharma-Pardharma (*Bhagvad Gita*), Spring-Pall. 'Nature' can broadly be interpreted to mean "those dark mossy labyrinths of the soul that languish for ever, hidden from the dazzling light of the sun." (*SCBB*) In simpler terms it means that voice or light which comes from within, from one's own inner world. It is fed and nourished by the age-old hills, valleys and mountains; the rivers and streams; the sun, the moon and the stars; rituals, songs and dances and so on. On the other hand, 'Culture' refers to the 'glossy surfaces of our pretensions' or that which comes from without through man-made systems and orders. It is shaped by the rational faculty of man through money, books, lectures and preachings.

Arun Joshi, an Indian novelist in English, in *The Strange Case of Billy Biswas* and Ngugi wa Thiong'o, an African novelist in English, in *The River Between* have consciously made use of these forces. Both the novelists have seriously tried to reveal that every man is born with his built-in Nature. Then as he grows, he should listen to, locate and follow this Nature which is a tough task. Very few people venture to do this and all the rest are led astray by culture. These rare people are Billy in *The Strange Case of Billy Biswas* and Wayaki, Muthoni, Nyambura in *The River Between*. These are the fortunate few claimants to a happy life; but the fact remains that they suffer and meet a sad end owing to the dominance of the culture world and the dearth of decisive direction from within.

The setting is clear and simple in both the novels. The life is seen flowing two streams in *The Strange Case of Billy Biswas*, viz. Harlem, the slum area inhabited by the black people, and the white world of the rich and the cultured in New York; the hill areas of the tribe in Orissa and Madhya Pradesh and the posh societies of Delhi and Bombay. In *The River Between*, it is seen along two ridges, viz. Kameno and Makuyu with a valley between them through which flows Honia river, the soul of the two ridges, throbbing and murmuring an unknown song. Kameno is inhabited by the tribe whose blood and bones speak the language of the hills and which has kept its magic and rituals pure and intact. Makuyu, on the other hand, is occupied by the white people, the missionaries unknown to the language of the hills and the ways of the land.

The primitives in *The Strange Case of Billy Biswas* are represented by Dhunia and Bilasia, while the civilized ones by the Biswases and the Chaterjees. Between the two stands Billy, born and brought up in the world of culture, but deeply drawn into the world of Nature. Similarly, Mr. Livingstone and Joshua in *The River Between* represent the world of Culture, while Chege and Kabonyi belong to the world of Nature. Between these two are caught Wayaki, Muthoni and Nyambura. Wayaki, the son of Chege, is deeply drenched in the primitive ways of life. He is also drawn to what is good in the white people. Muthoni and Nyambura, the daughters of Joshua, a converted Christian priest, are born and brought up in the new faith, but they are deeply rooted in the primitive ways of life. Both the novelists in the select novels have tried to peep into the inner world of such sandwiched characters as Billy, and Wayaki, Muthoni and Nyambura and very vividly depict their search, their struggle and their ventures to grab their goal.

Billy in *The Strange Case of Billy Biswas* keeps striving and struggling to fit into the frame of the material civilized world. But then he has the 'first glimpse of the other side.' In response to Tuula's question, he says, "most of us are aware of the side on which we are born, but there is always the other side, the valley beyond the hills; the hills beyond the valley." (19) Later he refers to this fact again in his talk to his father in the party: "All I am saying is that there are worlds at the periphery of this one, above it and below it, of which we know nothing until we are in them." (54) And when Mr. Biswas, his father, asks him how one gets into them, Billy simply says: "I don't know, something happens, something strange . . . and you are catapulted into them."

Billy himself came to know about his living link with the other side, when he was around fourteen and had been to Bhubaneswar, then an undeveloped sleepy town, with his mother. It was here in this tribal belt that it occurred to him that something had gone wrong with his life and that he belonged to that place. Until then he had been mostly in Delhi and Dehra Dun engaged in routine life like any other boy of his age. But here he felt his slumbering part getting suddenly awake. However, this spell was quickly shattered, when he returned to his normal civilized self in Delhi and Dehra Dun. He then has his first lapse at the age of twenty two in George's apartment in America at a party where he plays a pair of bongo drums. This process of awakening is further accelerated by his choice to study anthropology. And when Romi asks why he chose anthropology, he says:

> I don't really know, I am afraid. What I do know is that this is what I have always wanted to read (pointing to the books). All I want to do in life is to visit the places they (those books) describe, meet the people who live there, find out the aboriginalness of the world. (14)

Further, whenever he returned from his expeditions to the tribal areas, he couldn't shake off the sounds and smells of the forest for days together. Even at the climactic stage, he clearly heard the call first from a furry little animal and later from Bilasia to finally enter their world. And Billy, the son of a Supreme Court judge, ultimatelly offers himself to the primitive world.

However, even his metamorphosis as a primitive couldn't stabilize him. It is evident from what he says to Romi: "I was afraid that after all this upheaval I may still not have found the place where I really wanted to be." (148) Billy gradually realizes that "becoming a primitive was only a first step—a means to an end" and that he is "still seeking something else." And when Romi asks him whether that 'something' is 'God,' Billy simply says, "Something like that." (189) Thus Billy is out to strive, to seek and to realize the vision at the call of his conscience, though the form of this vision is not clearly visible to him.

Thus Billy is on the horns of a dilemma, that is, he fervently feels to follow his 'vision' or 'hallucination' springing spontaneously from within, but then its form 'Swarup' is not clear; he also strives hard to get adjusted in the civilized world, but then it gives less pleasure and more pain and provocation. The culture world of the Biswases and the Chaterjees doesn't satisfy him. The "finely dressed men and women seated on downy sofas" appear to him "a kennel of dogs yawning and snuggling against each other, or holding whisky glasses in their furred paws." (96) To Billy civilization is nothing more than making and spending of money. Even the so-called philosophers and thinkers appear hired to find solution or throw light on complications caused by this making and spending of money. He patently perceives the sham of this world. Even the beautiful women like Meena (his wife) and Rima (his fan) of the butterfly society fail to keep him long in their fold. To him living in this world was "foolish, squandering the priceless treasure of his life on that heap of tinsel that passed for civilization." (141)

On the other hand, as stated earlier, Billy starts feeling 'something inside him' as he grows in years. Tuula, a Swedish girl taking advanced training in psychiatric social work and Billy's intellectual friend, calls it "a great force, Urkraft a . . . a primitive force." (23) Initially Billy fails to perceive the nature of this inner stirring. But gradually it occurs to him that he is one of the primitives to be investigated and not one of the investigators. The last blow to cut Billy off from his thirty years of past comes from Bilasia, his second wife and with whom he has psycho-physical relations. He puts his experience of that crucial encounter with Bilasia as follows:

> Bilasia, at that moment, was the essence of that primitive force that had called me night after night, year after year. It was that that had drawn me to Tuula, to the study of anthropology, to the bizarre spots of North central America. (142)

Finally Billy becomes a primitive. It is also noted that this enormous volte face doesn't offer what he has searched for all these years. The culture force, at this delicate point, raises its head by making him feel guilty for what he has done. He even decides to go back to his wife, child and parents. But then this second voice is for ever silenced by his temple experience where he felt "as though I was in the presence of fate. I knew, I would never be able to leave these hills alive." (134) Thus once and for all he retreats to the primitive world obeying the dictates of his 'soul' and paying the highest price, viz. first the luxuries, then the prestigious job (the lecturership in the university Dept.), his parents, wife and child and above all his own life.

The theme of *The Strange Case of Billy Biswas* is also present in *The River Between* with some crucial variations. Chege, fully absorbed in the ways and laws of the tribe, takes his son Wayaki to the sacred grove, a place where Gikuyu and Mumbi, the parents of the tribe, had stood long ago. Then he tells him about the prophecy by Mugo, the ancestor, viz. "There shall come a people with clothes like butterflies" and "salvation shall come from the hills." And then he asks Wayaki: "Arise, hear the prophecy. Go to the mission place, learn all the wisdom and all the secrets of the white man. But do not follow his vices. Be true to your people and ancient rites." (20) It is this command that injects an element of fear and anxiety not only in Wayaki but also in him. He sends his son to Siriana, but later on turns suspicious about the final outcome: "Would he be corrupted by Siriana?" He also questions the wisdom of having sent his son to the mission place and wonders whether he would be punished like Joshua. (54)

Wayaki, initially, is fully in tune with the traditions of the tribe and the hymns of the hills. On the occasion of Initiation, we hear him say: "He was of the tribe." He had to endure its ways and be inside "the secrets of the hills." (46) He considers circumcision as important ritual to the tribe that has kept people together, bound the tribe, given meaning to a man's life. He also undergoes the ritual. But then his going to Siriana Mission School, gathering and absorbing ideas and notions from the new culture instill in him the element of conflict. This prevents him from responding spontaneously to the dances and celebrations at the initiation occasion. When other young men and women are in full frenzy of dances, Wayaki feels uneasy. Something inside him stops him from losing himself in that frenzy. However, he fails to locate what prevented him from doing so—Muthoni or "the Chaos created by locked emotions let loose?" (42) Further we also hear him say: "a feeling that he lacked something, that he yearned for something beyond him, came in low waves of sadness." (44)

Wayaki, now tall and powerfully built, finds himself outside Kameno-Makuyu rifts. But at intervals he feels isolated. He feels hungry and yearns for something that will feed him whole, that will take possession of the whole of himself. But that something seems "beyond him enmeshed in the ways of the land." (69) What is this longing for—His younger sister, who died early and whom he loved so much? Muthoni, whose soft but strong hold he had experienced at the dance? Right and unity of the hills and their people? The clear edges of life are lost. He doesn't see a way out. One night he comes out of his hut. The moon is awake, the whole ridge and everything wears a brilliant white. Here in these moments, he wants 'to feel one with the whole creation, with the spirits of his sister and father'—and again becomes restless and the yearning comes back to him. (72)

Then he suddenly realizes that he yearns for "Freedom," what we call 'Moksha' in our language. His new vision is "Education Unity. Political freedom." (142) But then this is closely linked with Nyambura. As he says: "He would fight for unity and Nyambura was an integral part of that battle. If he lost Nyambura, he too would be lost. He was fighting for his salvation." (143) He also views and reviews and ruminates over a series of questions: whether he has remained 'uncontaminated' by the ways of the white man as wished by his father. Whether the education he was trying to spread in the ridges is not a contamination. Whether he was trying to create order and bring light in the dark. Whether he really wants unity between Kameno-Makuyu or he is doing it for Nyambura. He also has a vision of "a people who could trust one another, who would sit side by side, singing the song of love which harmonised with music from the birds, and all their hearts would beat to the rhythm of the throbbing river." (120)

Muthoni, the younger daughter of Joshua, rebels first against the new faith. One day she tells Nyambura: "I want to be circumcised." (25) Further when Nyambura cautions her about the fact that how their father will be cross with her and how "they are now a Christian, wise in the ways of the white people," Muthoni boldly says that she wants to be "a woman, a real girl, knowing all the ways of the hills and ridges" and firmly declares: "the white man's God doesn't quite satisfy me. I want, I need something more. My life and your life are here in the hills." (26) She doesn't simply say this but also translates into action by running away to her aunt and actually participating in the ritual of circumcision. Further when Wayaki asks why she ran away from her father, she says: "No one will understand. I say I am a Christian and my father and mother have followed the new faith. I have not run away from that. But I also want to be initiated into the ways of the tribe." (44) Here it is quite evident that Muthoni is caught between two loyalties, viz. loyalty to her father's faith and to that of her own passed on to her from the ages-old hills and customs through her parents. Even while dying she says, "I am still a Christian, see, a Christian in the tribe" and finally asks Wayaki to tell Nyambura: "I see Jesus. And I am a woman, beautiful in the tribe." (53)

Joshua's elder daughter Nyambura finds it difficult to rebel against her father. She always finds him at the back of her. And yet she "wishes to rebel," but feels that she doesn't have her sister Muthoni's courage. (114) However, inwardly she realizes:

> that she could never be saved by Christ; that the Christ who died could only be meaningful, if Wayaki was there for her to touch,

> for her to feel and talk to. She could only be saved through Wayaki. He then was her saviour, her black Messiah, the promised one who would come and lead her into light. (103)

And ultimately she does collect courage and rebels against her father. One day Wayaki comes to Joshua's house to inform about some conspiracy against him. Joshua takes it as a lie and asks him to get out of his house. At this crucial moment, Nyambura cries out: "Teacher! come back." (135) She takes Wayaki's hand firmly and says: "O, teacher, I have always loved you. I will go where you go. Don't leave me now." (137)

The whole discussion can now be summed up thus:

i) The protagonists in both the novels are out in search of "something" or "salvation" or "light" inspired by their Nature. But then that 'something' is fluid and vague. Consequently they go on shifting the objects of their search. Naturally their journey becomes a prolonged pursuit of soap bubbles blown in the air. Billy in *The Strange Case of Billy Biswas* moves on thus: Tuula ⇒ anthropology ⇒ Meena ⇒ Rima Bilasia⇒ ? When the intrigued Romi asks Billy what he had been doing with himself those past ten years as a primitive, his plain reply is, "well, the fact is that I don't know. At times I put the question to myself and find that I haven't really got much to say for myself." (140) The same is the case with Wayaki in *The River Between*. He, too, goes on shifting thus: his younger sister, now dead ⇒ Muthoni ⇒ the spirit of his father ⇒ unity and education of the tribe ⇒ Nyambura ⇒ ? Muthoni mistakes that 'something' or 'salvation' for circumcision and Nyambura for Wayaki. All of them are searching the salvation out. Arun Joshi and Ngugi wa Thiong'o have, somehow, missed the fact that the real salvation has been seen not outside but in realization of the self as it is said in *Swetaswatar Upanishad*:

> Yatheiv bimbam mradyopliptam,
> tejomayam bhrajate tatsudhantam
> tadwatmtatwam prasmikshdehi
> Ekahkratartho bhavate weetsokah

ii) Both the novelists have corroborated the validity of what is said in *Bhagvad Gita*:

Sreyan swadharmo vigunah, pardharmatswanusthitat
Swadharme nidhanamsreyah, pardharmo bhayavah

That is, one should follow one's own inner voice (swadharma) whatever it might be at any cost, and that following Pardharma (the faith of others) leads to fear and insecurity. Billy listens to his inner voice. When Romi asks him whether he is sure about the voice of his soul, Billy firmly says, "Do you think I could have paid such a heavy price had it not been correct?" (186) For this inner voice he gives up not only the luxuries but also his life. Simiarly, Wayaki, Muthoni and Nyambura in *The River Between* are at their best when they listen to the inner self and when they don't, they are filled with fear and anxiety.

iii) The two novelists have differed in one crucial respect. Arun Joshi has not talked of or tried any compromise between these two worlds of Nature and Cultures. Billy feels the stirrings of Nature and he acts accordingly. He fights out the forces of culture. Finally he prefers to get killed by the representatives of culture instead of joining them. Billy doesn't attain the blissful state but is not divided either. Ngugi wa Thiong'o, on the other hand, attempts to achieve a compromise in *The River Between*. Chege, the champion of the tribe, sends his son to Siriana Mission School to learn the wisdom of the white man. And this act makes him suffer from suspicion and guilt. Muthoni, the daughter of the converted Christian priest, joins the ritual of circumcision at the behest of her inner voice. But then she also believes in her father's faith and sees Christ while dying. The conflicting loyalties bring her division and death. Wayaki's suffering also stems from his dual faith. The experiment hasn't proved worthwhile.

Ayi Kwei Armah's *Fragments*: The Dilemma of the 'been-to'

USHA BHATNAGAR

I lay the other night and dreamt
That we were all being glazed
With a white clay of foreign education,
And it was stifling, stifling the sleeping black man
Inside there.

Jonathan Kariara

Ayi Kwei Armah's novel *Fragments* begins with Baako and Brempong's return from the whiteman's country, the fancy land abroad. They land at the Ghana airport together. Baako alights timidly with his few possessions i.e. a suitcase, a typewriter and a guitar whereas Brempong walks out of the lounge with his head puffed up with the pride of being a 'been-to' and his hands full of expensive gifts. Brempong is the prototype of the neo-colonial blackman who, having been subjected to years of humiliation and insult at the hands of a supposedly culturally superior and politically formidable master, rejects his own identity and takes to mindless imitation of aliens. He cowers before white arrogance and in a desperate bid to pull up his sinking morale puts on a white mask. He is, most often, not accepted as equal by the 'master culture.' But for those who have not been blessed to cross over to the land of fancy, the 'been-to' is an icon of whiteman's virtues. He is accorded an elevated status because he has been to the envied land and has brought back relics of his prosperity.

A crowd of expectant friends and relatives gathers at the airport to receive Brempong, the returning 'been-to.' The 'been-to' son of the soil must not soil his boots in the soil of the African land. So, the sister spreads her cloth for the VIP brother to tread upon. The eager crowd throngs the transformed son but the sister shouts a reprimand that the precious brother should not be irritated by unhealthy tribal proximity.

> Move back, you villagers. . . . Don't come and kill him with your T.B. He has just returned and if you don't know let me tell you. The air where he has been is pure, not like ours.

The black man Brempong, returning from the magic land of the whites, sheds off his black identity and accepts the whiteman's VIP status without any reservations. The native crowd acclaims the transformation and endorses the new found alien identity of their son.

The identity deception would not be unconquerable if it were limited to only the less fortunate ones who, caught up in the survival struggle, look upon their converted son as their dream saviour. The crisis deepens because the educated 'been-to' is insensitive to the damage to his real self and succumbs, with a willing haste, to the illusion of his metamorphosis. Gratified with his self assumed integration into a 'superior culture,' he conjures up an unabashed display of his prosperity to authenticate his inflated identity. He alienates himself from the unblessed ones of his community as an additional assertion of his conversion to celebrity status. The blackman inside is stifled and life is measured from now onwards on an alien scale. The native food irritates the 'been-to's' palate, the native wine tastes horrid. The local perfume smells bad and the native dresses are unclassy. The 'been-to' rejoices in his slavish imitation of the colonial masters and the unsuccessful natives view his gimmicks with unconcealed envy. Riding high on the crest of borrowed glory of the whites the 'been-to' busies himself with the phoney fanfare of his cargo, the expensive things he carries with him. Naana, the old woman, who has been a witness to the old and the new, says:

> Things of beauty so great that I thought then in my soul this was the way the spirit land must be. Only it was a beauty that frightened also. (11)

Naana is frightened, in her vision to see the 'things of beauty' the travellers carry. These kill the soul and demolish the identity of the traveller. Derek Wright attributes the trend to colonialism:

> In Armah's fictional polemic cargoism is not an emanation from traditional faith but is tied up with colonial legacies.[2]

> Postcolonial cargoism erected around new black gift bringers . . . are more slavishly worshipful in their attitude towards white values and are more truly degraded in their undignified dependency upon the west.[3]

As the harbinger of wealth and status, Brempong is the fulfilment of family dreams. He walks tall and arrogant, like his colonial masters, for he brings his family deliverance from commonness and lifts them into an enviable position. Little does he realize that the carrier of things is metaphorically the carrier of his corpse.

> It is clearly understood that the been-to has been chosen, been awarded a certain kind of death. A beneficial death since cargo follows his return. Not just cargo but also importance, power, a radiating influence capable of touching ergo elevating all those who, in the first instance, have suffered the special bereavement caused by the been-to's going away. (157)

On the other hand Baako, returning home in the changed social cultural spectrum, feels unsure of himself. In a society where 'been-to' is the pass word to success, Baako, who returns home with no possessions except his dreams for his mother country, is apprehensive of being a disappointment to his people.

He lingers on, a while, in Paris to defer his reunion with his people as a failure. Paris is the symbolic space that Baako temporarily discovers for himself between the alien white world where he was an isolated misfit and his native Africa which demands a new role from him. The dread of his family's dreams slows his pace. He realizes:

> That everything he had done in about the last half year had been intended as a postponement, a pushing away of things to which he felt necessarily called. (6)

Baako's stay in Paris is a wilful suspension of time. The present is used as a means to leave behind the past and also to postpone the future. The past zooms on with wasteful expansion and the future holds no promise to the stranded traveller. Aimless movement of Baako in Paris parallels the absence of a target in his life. The undecided Baako resembles the North African

> who is pushing bits of papers aimlessly along the flat gutter with a broom of twigs. (7)

The purposeless indulgence of the North African is an emphatic duplication of the aimless wanderings of Baako in Paris. The North African stands out as a statement of loneliness and uncertainties of the Africans who are sent out to alien lands with unreal hopes and expectations.

Suspension of time and space is followed by a conscious shutting off of the unsavoury engulfing reality. Since the world is too powerful to be shut out, the individual shuts himself in. Basic to it is the desire to evade the imminent. Baako is drawn "by an intense interest in what the man was doing in his shut off world." (8)

At the Ghana airport Baako watches the boisterous welcome accorded to Brempong. The spectacle leaves him dubious and sceptical about his stance and he sneaks out stealthily. The disquietitude enforces another postponement in the series of many and Baako takes a room in a hotel for the night. Brempong's pretensions and the exuberant cheering of the crowd haunt him with questions:

> He saw the darkness inside his head filling with the sweating, smiling, suited figure of Brempong caught happily in the centre of the crowd. . . . He was sure there was a wall between him and Brempong. Maybe the man could see something he was blind to or maybe he had eyes denied to the exhilarated Brempong. (62)

Analyzing the state of mind of Baako, Robert Fraser says:

> Superficially Baako's anxiety is that of any sensitive youngman returning to his own country after a prolonged spell abroad; he is worried about whether he can face upto the role now expected of him. But in Baako's case the source of worry is complicated by his exact awareness of those cultural factors which will have moulded his family's probable reaction to him. In his absence the inarticulate longings of his family will have weaved themselves into a tight web of expectations which threaten him on his arrival.[4]

Baako needs a place of seclusion to get a breathing respite from the onrush of anxiety. The loneliness of the hotel room is welcome to him because "He felt an ambiguous comfort, savouring the sense of being so alone back home connected for the moment to nobody." (64) But time moves on and the dreaded moment arrives. Baako's mother sobs, trembles and collapses at the suddenness of her reunion with the departed son. Baako is back with the promise of the deeply coveted comforts. The pleasure of gaining a proud status thrills the mother. Sitting in the car of Baako's friend,

> She was smiling now, completely at ease in the enfolding luxury of the red leather upholstery.
>
> She was asking in a near whisper filled with wonder and gladness, "when is yours coming Baako?"
>
> "What" he asked surprised.
>
> "Yours, your car so that my old bones can rest." (70)

Fraser, explaining the desires of the mother, says: "The mother's dreams are born out of a profound longing for release. Baako is the child who has been sent away to forge the weapons of deliverance." (33)

The returning 'been-to,' in most cases, is as much a prey to the falsities as those who await him and his movements are monitored by certain pre-determined conceptions like that of a mechanical toy. Baako refuses to follow the predecided mechanics. He has brought with him dreams for his country. He is impatient to communicate these to the masses. Working with Ghanavision, Baako picks up films as the medium to convey his vision to the people "as a way of making my life mean something to me." (80) But at Ghanavision, there are no takers for his scripts. Ghanavision is monopolized by power maniacs and opportunistic psychophants who have turned the media into a praisesinging instrument for those who hold power. "His idealistic hope to revitalize Ghana through creative journalism at Ghanavision is a mirage." (61)

During his search for the creative medium, Baako's visit to the drama studio reveals appalling facts. Akosua Russel, the editor of the prestigious magazine 'Kyerema,' is more proficient in collecting American money than in creative writing and others who hang around her are equally deft at the game.

Baako shares his shock with Ocran, the art teacher, but the teacher has learnt the wisdom of compromise as he has been a helpless witness to several malpractices. Ocran understands Baako's restlessness at the alarming turn of events. He shares his anxiety yet he warns him: "If you want to do any work here you have to decide quite soon that you'll work alone." (81) Baako, who is sensitive to the misdirection of his country, finds himself alone as if in a wilderness. Baako, who scorned at the elite isolation of the 'been-to,' is confronted with the helpless isolation of the impotent. Ghana is a world sunk in moral morass and a return to the roots is like digging your own grave. Lawrence Boateng, like Baako, refuses to submit to the political and social artifice. He is harrowed by an entire gaggle of self important people who are out to invent tools for self gratification only. Checkmated, he drowns his defeat in heavy drinking. Beer after beer and impotent and unheeded protestations is all that remains of the visionary and his visions. The societies are fragmented into familial units intent upon self-preservation. The collective welfare has no place in the individualistic scheme of things. The traditions which regulated the frenzy for personal gain have been discarded under western influence to be replaced by untrammelled lust for individual success.

Gariba, another victim of the sterility of the times and 'destruction of worth,' constantly reminds Baako that acceptance is the only way to survive. It is impossible in the present set up to bring awareness to the people that beauty and strength are wasted in the absence of direction. The success loving 'been-tos' accept the pretensions and soon become a part of the decadence. In this scenario of messed up values, when Baako makes a decision to revive the beautiful, he invites upon himself the predicament of the lonely fighter.

> In the new Ghana where the possession of objects testifies the status and identity of a person, the nurse, before taking in Araba who is due to deliver, verifies Baako's status who brings his sister to the hospital.
>
> "Are you a senior officer? This new wing is for V.I.P.s and senior officers." (75)

Baako has turned down the V.I.P. status. Hence he must suffer at the hands of the system. Baako is restive to reconstruct the system and looks forward to the rebirth of his country. The birth of Araba's baby can be taken as representative of the emergence of a new Ghana—the revival of the dead times. But the baby is stifled in the folds of rich clothes by the strong draft of the 'wind machine' and so is the new Ghana. Baako's desperation to save the baby is symbolic of his panic to free his country from the destructive clutches of neocolonialism and materialistic mood. Robert Fraser says:

> In effect the episode and the death of the child which results can be seen as an extended metaphor of the factors which the novelist sees as strangling the nation's intellectual life. (39)

Human relationships, both in personal and public life, are gauged on financial parametres. "Efua, Baako's mother, exploits her friends in order to make her grandson's outdooring ceremony profitable for the family."[5] Human life is rendered insignificant. Flight above and away from the ordinary man's pain on the 'been-to' wings has become the way of life. The Public Works Engineer advises an agitated Baako: "You know sure way of avoiding the mess. Why don't you fly?" (140) Those who refuse to fly on the V.I.P. wings are doomed to a life of helpless agony and anguish. Baako's choice to stay with the masses and make others see the truth from behind their V.I.P. masks, seals his fate. Baako's commitment is understood neither at Ghanavision nor at home.

> He finds himself alienated from his society by its open and cynical corruption and from his family by their inability to understand that his ambitions are not primarily material ones. (25)

Baako's alienation originates from his desire to reject dependence on colonial legacies. He fervently tries to re-establish contacts with his people but his attempts towards re-assimilation are scoffed at as abnormal. He is castigated and chased like a rabid dog. Baako is "filled with a strange frustrated anger." (133) It is the anger of the impotent who can see his failure against the massive rottenness, stinking yet powerful. Baako's desperation to point out the stink to the masked faces is dismissed as mad and absurd. To escape the stress of frustration, Baako decides to shut himself into a personal world of his own. He, now, creates visions within his mind for himself alone. The routed fighter seeks hiding in a closed-in reality to avoid metaphoric death outside. But the shut off strategy fails to ease the anguish of the sufferer. The escape is unsuccessful and momentary. Baako is admitted into a mental hospital as demented and deranged—a case of mental aberration.

At the end of the novel, the journey has come full circle, the cycle is complete. The novel ends with the same psychological confusions and misgivings that it opened with. At the outset, Baako lingered at the edges, wandered away in Paris, hesitated to enter the shambolic Ghana, he is back at the edges as the story concludes. Baako closes himself into an impenetrable world of his own. The insulated world may be invulnerable to the chaos outside, but it offers no escape from the pain inside. Baako's isolation signals his surrender but it is not the thoughtless surrender of Brempong to the pyromaniac paradise of individual success. Brempong's success is a sign of the ultimate ruin whereas Baako's defeat promises eventual reversal of social trends.

Baako is nettled in the lopsided struggle with the gigantic forces of decadence. He is checkmated yet he remains unvanquished. His discomfiture is frustrating but it is a beacon light to the stranded. The defeated Baako's unrelenting and uncompromising war against the colonial legacy is a promise of new times, whereas the apparent win of Brempong is an abysmal fall into nothingness. The lonely 'been-to' stands as a warning against the shame which demolished Africa's dignity. The shame may recur if the call of the visionary fighter remains unresponded to

This story of disgrace and shame shows up in nearly all those countries which were liberated from the colonial rule after the II world war.

The Brempong of *Fragments* is Lateef in the Canadian writer M.G. Vassanji's *All Worlds Are Possible Now*. The dollar earning Lateef hopping easily from Canada to Saudi Arabia and to Dar in Tanzania is messiah for the local African and Asian boys and the narrator who comes back home to reclaim his identity is Baako the philistine: "But for this his old school . . . he [Lateef] is the messiah and I the philistine."[6]

The dream of the world beyond is carried forward by the people returning from there. Their flamboyant and unashamed display of their materialistic possessions is an effort to retain their privileged status. Their euphoric and happy cries about the great world are a sad reminder to the less fortunate ones of what they lack.

> Shadowy cargo vessels cheerlessly ply these waters, bringers of unaffordable goods, reminders of deprivation, enticements to get up and go. (130)

The African 'been-to' is a counterpart of the 'foreign returned' Indian of the neo-colonial age. The predicament is shared by all the new colonial societies. The political liberation from a demoralizing alien power does not ensure mental emancipation. For these societies, bereft of pride, west continues to be the land of their unrealized dreams. The been-to stands as a fragile liaison around which the colonized minds weave the fancy fabric of their lives. They willingly surrender to the falsities of colonial mirage and submerge their 'being' into it. The surrender, a signature of cultural complex, writes the annihilation of a race.

The been-to temperament is a colonial legacy. Dennis Lee, in the context of Canada, calls it "inward colonization." The recovery has to commence inversely. The been-to has to discover his tongue to redeem his lost self pride and demolished identity. In the words of Ngugi:

> In my view language was the most important vehicle through which that power fascinated and held the soul prisoner. The bullet was the means of the physical subjugation. Language was the means of spiritual subjugation.
>
> Language, any language, has a dual character; it is both a means of communication and a carrier of culture.[7]

The "words of home" (Lee) have the magic to revive ancient wisdom and to discover the historical being. The colonial societies, then, will not beseech western confirmation of 'I exist.'

The dilemma of the been-to is not situational alone. It is implanted in the mind of the colonial man. The been-to needs to grapple with his complexes that blinker his vision and block his view of his absurd existence. He belongs to nowhere. He leads a schizophrenic life. The impersonating personality dominates the real one but, occasionally, when the real being surfaces, an unbearable isolation overwhelms the man. The dilemma can be resolved only by decolonizing the mind. As Leopold Senghor says,

> O bless this people, Lord, who seek their own face under the mask and can hardly recognize it.[8]

NOTES

1. Ayi Kwei Armah, *Fragments* (Boston: Houghton Muffin, 1970), p. 59.
2. Derek Wright, *Ayi Kwei Armah's Africa—The Sources of his Fiction* (London: Munich, New York: Hans Zell, 1989), p. 166.
3. Derek Wright, "*Fragments*, The Cargo Connection," *Kunapipi*, 7, 1 (1985), p. 46.
4. Robert Fraser, *The Novels of Ayi Kwei Armah* (London, Ibadan: Heinemann, 1980), p. 53.
5. Edward Lobb, "Armah's *Fragments* and the Vision of the Whole," *ARIEL*, Vol. 10, No. 1 (Jan. 1979), p. 28.
6. M.G. Vassanji, *Uhuru Street* (McClelland & Stewart, 1992), p. 134.

7. Ngugi wa Thiong'o, *Decolonizing the Mind* (Zimbabwe Publishing House, 1987), p. 13.
8. Hosties Noires, Paris, January 1945.

Buchi Emecheta's *Gwendolen*: An Affirmation of Life-Force

B. INDIRA

Buchi Emecheta's *Gwendolen* is a raging commentary on inequality of sexual relationships. However, the novelist moves farther to prove a point—that a woman is no longer confined to a deplorable dependency on man or for that matter another woman. All this in the life of a mere sixteen-year-old girl. From an accursed childhood extending into adolescence, Gwendolen rises above any accepted pattern to give birth to her father's child. Here is a life of excruciating agony—from a timid, self-conscious five-year-old trying to hide away her shame from the glaring sunlight by resorting to bed wetting to the confident, proud mother of Iyamide.

Who are the villains in little Gwendolen's life, if one may ask so. Mammy and papa, who can never even pronounce her name properly and who leave her to fend for herself from a tender age of five? Or the grandmother who feels deprived of her boyfriend and his help as Gwendolen dares to expose his true colours? Or is it Uncle Johnny who helps Gwendolen out of her mother's womb and yet crawls surreptitiously into her tiny bed night after night in sexual avarice after he has had his share with the grandmother?

Uncle Johnny snatches away Gwendolen's world of innocence from her. For him it is sex without any risk whereas for Gwendolen it's one big confusion, shame and guilt as she is bullied into repeated sexual assaults. The little girl is too young to realize that in Uncle Johnny's stealthy act lies her destiny. If the act of sex is supposed to turn a girl into a woman, Gwendolen is brutally displaced from her cradle and forced into womanhood at a tender age of seven. Neither a child nor an adult, unable to comprehend the implications of the act, she is left utterly defenseless in that despicable world. Eversince, her body has not been hers. Uncle Johnny does not miss any opportunity to further alienate Gwendolen from her parents and exploits her helplessness. He tries to make her believe time and again that he is the only one who can look after her. The shy child who wages a silent rebellion at the mother's departure, "a final act of rejection," (18) is left repeating helplessly in pain and perplexity: "Mammy, why. . . ?" (22) Besides there is the immense fear of being blamed if she were to reveal the old man's sexual buffoonery since Uncle Johnny has successfully convinced people around that he has been looking after the little girl.

Gwendolen's tender brain forever fails to discern the real Uncle Johnny—there is a day-time Uncle Johnny with nothing but a grandfather's love for Gwendolen and the night time one. Paralysed by fear and embarrassment, the child-stoic passively puts up with the emotional fatigue. Her bed-wetting intensifies. The granny worries only about the stinking bed whereas for Gwendolen it is a "perpetual load." (27)

The neighbourly suggestion of consulting a doctor panics Gwendolen: what if he were to discover? She runs away to her dad's people. Though it is a futile trip, Gwendolen picks up courage to part with her hateful secret. Uncle Johnny dismisses it as Gwendolen's imagination. The men-folk laugh at her. They all mistrust her and try to prove her wrong. Though the women react with a certain warmth, their daughters are strictly warned to keep away from the evil one. Granny feels cheated by her boyfriend. Gwendolen understands that adults indulge in a lot of lying. She wonders why she did not bite Uncle Johnny all these days when Cocoa hints at it during a secret meeting. Uncle Johnny is now prohibited from entering their surroundings.

Gradually, as money stops coming in from England, and as Uncle Johnny is forced into withdrawing his help in bee-cultivation, granny who once vibrated to Gwendolen turns indifferent to her. She openly condemns Gwendolen's swaying of hips and other body movements as meant to provoke men. After all, it is not Uncle Johnny's fault, she concludes. The eleven-year-old girl now is impatient to go to England not because her parents live there but because a new place may help her in establishing a new identity for herself, away from Uncle Johnny and bed-wetting.

She travels from Granville, her native village in West Indies, to England on her own at the behest of the parents. Throughout the journey, Gwendolen is haunted by the question, what if? As the aircraft reaches its destination, she embraces the air-hostess in an act of love and trust. That is her last attempt to touch the world of Granville and the umbilical cord is now cut. Dressed in father's big coat which she believes can conceal her secret, she reaches out to her father who looks surprised and uneasy at her sudden youthful presence. In her excitement, Gwendolen cannot see that her father has to really work hard to revive his fatherly feelings towards her.

Once home,, Gwendolen rushes into her mother's open arms and feels reborn. She feels secure, "as if she was entering into her mother's womb again; new June-June." (52) The confident brothers and the baby sister whom she meets for the first time, and the father's physical presence reduce her to an outsider. As the rest of the family grows closer to her, the mother begins to treat her as a challenge. Gwendolen is a poignant reminder of Sonia's diminishing youth. Mother's piercing looks always targeted towards her growing youthful body embarrass Gwendolen. It takes her back to granny and Granville. There she had at least Shrivon and Cocoa to talk to. In the absence of any adequate communication between Gwendolen and her parents (Winston, stammering and stuttering is always reticent), she is once again pushed into a well of loneliness. Even school going ends in a disappointment—somehow it is shamefully reminiscent of Uncle Johnny. Though initially confused with the church, Gwendolen establishes some identity with it as her father preaches there.

When Sonia leaves for Jamaica at the unexpected news of her mother's ill-health, . Gwendolen assumes the role of a perfect little mother. The departure brings a sense of relief and freedom in her. Thrown into a closer proximity with the daughter, she becomes a nagging source of agony and guilt for Winston—he is constantly stirred by her beauty. He even obliquely discusses with his Nigerian colleague if one can marry one's daughter. Ilochina condemns it as a sin against the earth. He warns Winston that such a father is sure to be killed by the earth-force. But Winston feels that a father has a right over his daughter as he is responsible for her life. The daughter fades away from his mind and in her place he sees a well-shaped youthful flesh. The mother-surrogate becomes a sex-surrogate. What brought the father and the daughter together earlier now tears them apart. The bond of blood turns bloody. Gwendolen's paternal Eden snaps to ground.

For Winston Gwendolen has never been a daughter save the accidental physical bond. She is simply another woman to be desired (ironically both the mother and the daughter dress alike at the time of the mother's marriage). The pressure of physical desire wipes away the reasonable divide of I and the other in Winston's mind. His impulsions propel outwards.

Winston is irritated and angry to note that the daughter is not a virgin. He freezes time and self as he makes love to the daughter night after night for two years turning blind to the risk of destroying both her and himself in the process. The carnivorous arrogant brute in Winston finds a sexual guinea pig at no risk in a foreign country right under his own roof.

Winston watches helplessly at Gwendolen's bloating belly till she accidentally runs into Emannuel, a Greek boy. He indirectly encourages her into a relationship with the boy. Gwendolen turns coquettish to conceal her pregnancy. She goes to bed with her boyfriend with least consideration to the father in the adjoining room. The women at the Church and Ilochina suspect something terrible happening in Winston's home.

When Sonia returns, she is horrified at the state of affairs. She condemns the daughter and her boyfriend whom she believes to be the father of the child. Not only that, she threatens Emannuel's parents into accepting the fact. Winston as usual remains silent. Gwendolen does not contradict the mother nor does she try to defend the fact. However, Sonia herself seems to be vaguely aware of the wretched happening in her absence. She confirms that the daughter is the evil one, out to destroy her and 'her' family. Her rivalry towards the daughter multiplies. The night Sonia returns to England, Gwendolen leaves home out of disgust as she hears the parental bed cringing and her mother grunting.

Gwendolen knows that Winston is incapable of extending any help to her. Several times she is tempted to shout: "But look dad, I am carrying your baby." (191) She knows that a mere hint regarding her pregnancy will disturb the world order around her family. She prepares herself to be mutilated and refuses to disclose the father's identity even to the police who pick her up from a park and later to the asylum authorities. Though she is found by the police in a state of shock, she neither feels disgraced of her condition nor does she regret it.

When the parents visit her at the asylum, Sonia is shocked by Winston's indifference towards the pregnant daughter. That is the last Gwendolen sees of him. Confirming Sonia's fears, Winston dies in a trap of gas and electricity considered part of the Earth forces. Embittered, Sonia stops visiting the daughter. From the asylum, Gwendolen is moved into a shelter home. She goes alone to give birth to the child. All along, only Emannuel remains as her support. She finally confesses to him that he is not the father of her child as accused by her mother. When Emannuel questions her about the father, her simple answer is that he is dead. Gwendolen and Emannuel go on to remain each other's succour. She goes out to attend her music classes while he baby-sits.

In Gwendolen's life, the anguish of separation especially from the mother is accentuated by the sudden violent sexual intercourse (Uncle Johnny used to gag her) with a man as old as her grandfather. At a time she is to amuse people with her child-antics, Gwendolen is forced into entertaining an old man with her flesh. She faces excommunication even from the granny for no fault of hers. Ever since it is an absurd, uncertain, incomprehensible world of evil darkness and urine-stench. The prospect of a secure family goes apiece with the antagonistic treatment of the mother. The father in his right turns the daughter into a passive victim to his parental eroticism. For Winston she is a sexual convenience in the absence of the wife. That Winston himself undergoes a host of psychic dangers is beside the point. The loving world of the parents, more so that of the father, crumbles down under the weight of Winston's animal gratification. And from the debris of a father's incest, a new Gwendolen springs forth. She gains a sense of personal bearing in life from the depth of her solitude to charter her course with "a sense of personal direction and independent awareness." Unshackling herself from the incessant maze of conflicts, fear, guilt and shame, Gwendolen becomes more involved in life as the proud mother of Iyamide which in Yoruba means, "My mother, my female friend, my female saviour, my anything nice-you-can-think-of-in-a-woman's form." (210)

NOTE

1. Buchi Emecheta, *Gwendolen* (Great Britain: Flamingo, 1989).

The Outsider in Mariama Ba's *Scarlet Song*

S. INDIRA

East is East and West is West: the twain shall never meet. Time and again, it has been manifested in Indian-English fiction. Kamala Markandaya's *Some Inner Fury* and Ruth Prawer Jhabvala's *Esmond in India* and a host of other novels serve as examples. The conflict in inter-racial marriages was claimed to be inevitable in colonial and postcolonial periods due to Western prejudices and Eastern incomprehension. But in the 80s when people in all societies were educated and refined enough to break the geographical and cultural barriers and look upon the world as one entity, Mariama Ba's novel *Scarlet Song*[1] comes as a shock.

Mariama Ba, a Sangalese writer, is known as a crusader against social injustices, waging a battle against the indignities inflicted on women. For social vision encompasses the plight of women and the immediate need for female self-awareness and a reexamination of values and attitudes dominant in the patriarchal African society. Both her novels *So Long a Letter* and *Scarlet Song* depict their woman protagonists as victims of polygamy, a patriarchal practice, sanctioned by Islam, a traditional religion. Both Ramatoulaye and Aissotou in *So Long a Letter* deal with polygamy stoically enough as it is a familiar evil. While Ramatoulaye resigns herself to her fate and remains the neglected first wife of her husband, Aissotou bravely walks out of marriage and becomes an independent individual, a bread-winner and a proud mother who could monitor her son's progress. On the other hand Mireille, the woman protagonist of *Scarlet Song* is totally crushed by the relentless power of polygamy as she is a white girl, a stranger to the inexorable grip of religion and tradition in African society.

Mireille, the daughter of a French diplomat Monsieur Jean, meets Ousmane, the son of a poor, invalid, exserviceman of Senegal, Djibril Gueye, at school. Drawn together by their mutual interest in philosophy and sharing similar critical attitudes, they fall in love. To Ousmane, Mireille is a princess, a spirit-bride, a daily presence in his dreams with her silky golden hair, graceful curves and milk-white body. She has dispelled Ousmane's mistrust of girls being flighty and irresponsible, ready to lie and deceive with their feminine wiles and seductive glimmers. She has become a source of inspiration to Ousmane, rebuilding his confidence which was shaken by the jeers and sneers of his childhood love, Ouleymatou.

Ousmane is thus dazzled by her beauty and intelligence. But Mireille's love for him is not prompted by any physical or psychological aberrations but is natural, genuine and spontaneous. She finds in Ousmane, intelligence and charm, the qualities she looked for in a partner. She believes in a love that knows no national frontiers. She knows she has taken a great risk but is determined to fight her way. When confronted by her father, she proudly proclaims her love for the black man, vehemently protesting against the father's pseudo-liberalism. Repelled by his true nature, the same old colonizer in the guise of a humanitarian, Mireille is all the more convinced that at least she shouldn't play the same game since she truly believes in the equality of all men. Helpless in the face of the thundering accusations and assertions of his daughter, Monsieur Jean packs her off to Paris, using his parental authority as she is yet a minor. Refusing to give up her love, Mireille is prepared to face the four years' exile in her country. Ousmane too on his part, waging a mental war against the clutches of his neighbourhood, his family and Africa itself with its unrelenting traditions, gives in to his youthful love, fanned by his illusory belief in himself that he can be both Mireille's husband and Yaya Khady's son at the same time. He affirms that he will never renounce his black identity for her sake but she should convert herself to Islam before becoming his wife. Mireille accepts all his uncompromising demands as she respects his resolve to retain his identity just as she is determined to affirm her own. She doesn't mind giving up her religion as she has no faith in it any longer. Reasoning out in the same way that they might be successful though the path laid out by their predecessors is too thorny to take risks, Mireille and Ousmane get married in Paris after five long years of waiting and preparation.

Like the fairytales, this intense romantic tale of Ousmane and Mireille does end in marriage but they do not live happily ever-after. Ousmane's friends' prophetic warning "Africa can be cruel in her jealously" (39) does come true. While Djibril Gueye accepts Mireille as a necessary "evil" (66) seeking solace in the religion which states that marriage is the result of divine intervention, Yaye Khady decides to fight against the she-devil, the Innee who has lured her son away from her. To her, Mireille is not a person but just an elusive film-star or an invisible spirit. She resents being deprived of her due as a mother-in-law, as a white girl can never fulfil the role of a black daughter-in-law who knows and respects the rights and privileges of a mother-in-law. Hundreds of years of subjugation to the white race resulting in suspicion, mistrust and fear of exploitation have left their mark in the very souls of black people. So, who can blame Yaye Khady, an illiterate woman for believing that the white woman manipulates her husband like "a puppet," (73) impoverishes the family by undermining its unity and so can't be integrated into the black community. She looks upon Mireille as an "usurper" (80) to be got rid of and she sets out to work briskly towards that end. Her hostility and continual surveillance of Mireille's doings have had the intended effect. Mireille is now considered by her husband to be "possessive and self-centred." (82) Even after Mireille gets her own flat, which she decorates tastefully, Yaye Khady continues to visit the couple at odd hours and triggers off a quarrel between them by spitting off her toothpicks on the carpet or doing some such malicious thing on purpose. The rift is further widened by Ousmane's childhood friends who drop in at all hours, staying on indefinitely, showing least consideration to Mireille and her way of life, goading Ousmane to be the master of the house, not to let himself to be dictated to or assimilated. To Mireille's dismay, Ousmane dismisses off her complaints and tears as meaningless, saying "When you marry a man, you also take on his life-style." (81) Thus he slips into the role of the traditional husband who allots a subservient role to the wife. Mireille, once his intellectual equal, the ideal companion, "the flaming torch lighting up his path" (84) has now become a nagging, unaccommodative, uncompromising wife. Her qualities and abilities which were admirable before, now seem to be typical of the westerners who dominated and exploited them; her meticulousness, cleanliness, her capacity to organize and classify things, her insistence on clear-cut views irritate and alarm Ousmane. Mireille suddenly becomes an outsider and a rival to be put in place. Hence, his outrageous conduct, shouting at Mireille to get out if she can't stand Yaye Khady's presence (95) and his total lack of sympathy and affection even when she collapses at his brutal outburst.

No longer the proud companion of her husband, Mireille is reduced to the ignominious status of a wife who would make all compromises in order to restore the harmony of her home. She tries to please her in-laws and Ousmane's cronies but her efforts at adaptation are met only with contempt. Her earlier courage and convictions seem to be deserting her at the continuous onslaught on her "self" and sense of identity. She feels she cannot resurrect herself as another woman, the kind of woman Ousmane wants while he himself considers any kind of compromise as surrender itself.

Alienated from his wife, ashamed at having sired a half-caste child, Ousmane falls an easy prey to the seductive appeal of Ouleymatou, forgetting his earlier experience with her. The illicit relationship gets an unspoken approval from the entire family of Ouleymatou purely for economic reasons. The generous bank notes given by Ousmane have silenced the voice of their conscience: Ousmane's success is the main reason even for Ouleymatou's scheming to seduce him and trap him into marriage. Everyone in the compound goes rapturous over Ouleymatou "Merchandise that had gone to the highest bidder," (135) at her son's baptism, bowled over by the sheer extravagance of the ceremony. Ousmane, on the other hand, justifies his deceit and double life by the pretext that he is lured back to his roots. Now Ouleymatou becomes his soulmate as they are linked by their common origins, the same ancestors, the same traditions and customs—"cultural justifications for what is simply a physical infatuation" (139) as his friend Ali rightly perceives. A silly, sensuous girl like Ouleymatou cannot possibly contribute to any positive guidance in his life. By seeking alliance with him, Ouleymatou has given a big boost to Ousmane's ego and he simply relishes being the lord and master at her house where his slightest whim is honoured with great respect. He sees his marriage with Mireille as a folly prompted by "the novelty of the Siren-Song that lured him." (150) He accepts that he was excited by the difficulty of enterprise, of being loved by a rich, refined white girl but once he achieves his goal, he has lost interest in it, it no longer fulfills his inner needs. The irony is, Ousmane, the "object" in the eyes of Monsieur Jean, treats his precious daughter precisely like "an object" to be easily expended. Does Ousmane intend this pitiless revenge against a girl who has given his everything without imposing any conditions? In a reversal of roles, it is he who is the racist now despite his rhetorical proclamations of anti-racism, just like his illiterate mother. His callousness towards Mireille's plight, ("Let her eat her heart out from neglect and boredom" [150]) and his deceit and treachery in keeping her in dark about his double life, in deciding that "the white woman must go" (150) reveal his racist tendencies. Glorifying his racism, he looks upon himself as "a fighter, an ambassador of his people" (150) and Ouleymatou as the symbol of Africa. His education has not helped him in being more human and tolerant, unfettered by racial prejudices.

It is Mireille who is the true anti-racist, a noble humanitarian in whom are reposed loyalty, love, courage and sacrifice. When she finally comes to know her husband's treachery, she feels disgusted with him and his family, a bunch of deceitful people with the exception of Soukeyna. Using all her resolve not to be crushed, not to be exploited by the prejudiced black society, Mireille tries to live bravely. But realising to her horror and dismay that she has become an "exile" in her own country, unacceptable to her parents with a black child, and "an unwanted outsider" in her adopted country. Mireille becomes paralysed with grief, fury and uncertainty. Ousmane's love letters written during their long courtship affirming his everlasting love mock cruelly at her. Sanity deserting her, she searches for her physical imperfections that have driven off Ousmane into the arms of the black woman. Flooded with nausea and resentment, she feeds her son with a fatal dose of sleeping tablets crying vehemently, "There's no place in this world for the Gnouloule Khessoole (not black, not white)—You, my child, you are going to leave this world." (165) She tries to attack a dazed Ousmane returning from Ouleymatou's place but he is saved. The dismal ending of the novel is thus the "scarlet song of lost hopes," (166) hopes of the West and the East coming together in love and understanding, making the world a better place to live in.

Racism seems to be such a cruel monster that no one, neither white, nor black nor coloured can escape its murderous grip. Some critics argue that the message in the novel is subverted with a strong undercurrent of sympathy for Ousmane and love and loyalty for everything African shown in the vibrant, colourful descriptions of Ouleymatou's dressing, cooking and her son's baptism.[2] But, nowhere does the writer condone the actions of Ousmane. Through the protesting voices of Ali, Rosali and Soukeyna, Mariama Ba lashes at Ousmane as a hypocrite who tried to hide under the canopy of religion using it as a cover for his male ego and black pride, ignoring its basic value—a generous heart, pity and charity—as taught by his pious father. The shameful truth that her husband prefers a subservient wife to an intellectual partner and that he has become the racist now drives Mireille mad as the very structure on which she has built her married life crumbles, jeering at her idealism, values, beliefs and hopes. Furious at this defeat as a person and as a wife, helpless at the tragic waste of her potential and her life, Mireille makes the demented move towards redemption, saving her son from the terrible fate of having "to live on the fringes of the two worlds destined never to meet" (124) that awaits him. Mireille's son if lived could have been the successor of Srinivas in Kamala Markandaya's *The Nowhere Man* and Baumgartner in Anita Desai's *Baumgartner's Bombay* who remained outsiders in their adopted countries even after fifty years of stay. *Scarlet Song* thus is an indictment against a sick society which cannot redress the imbalances, be they of race, colour or gender; encourage noble aspirations and nurture true love.

NOTES

1. Mariama Ba, *Scarlet Song* (England: Longman, 1981), trans. Dorothy Blair (Hongkong, New York: Longman, 1985).
2. Charles Ponnumhurai Sarvan, "Feminism and African Fiction: The Novels of Mariama Ba," *Modern Fiction Studies*, Volume 34, No. 3, Autumn 1988.

Conflict Between Cultures:
Ama Ata Aidoo's "Everything Counts"

G. SUDHAKAR

The political independence which became synonymous with the neo- colonialism posed a great threat to the richness and strength of native cultures of African countries. Absence of a coherent ideology and clear cut direction led the people to ape the alien life style. And the introduction of new education system became a powerful source to propagate the supremacy of western life over that of the natives.

Ama Ata Aidoo of Ghana is one of the committed female writers who marshalled her scathing criticism against the influence of western culture of African countries. She has a great commitment for blacks and their betterment. She reiterates "I feel a responsibility and I feel that its the same type of responsibility I think black people all over feel."[1]

In the story "Every thing Counts" in *No Sweetness Here*, Aidoo bitterly criticizes the imitation of the practice of 'wig-wearing' and the mad craze for cars and refrigerators by the blacks not only in her country but also in the other countries of Africa.

The protagonist Sissie in the story goes to a university to pursue higher education. There she encounters many an African woman who tries to look like white girls by straightening their hair. In the vacation Sissie visits some of the African Countries. To her surprise, she notices there wigs and stylish hair cuttings of the women ranging from air-stewardesses to the grade three typists in the offices. Later, at the time of festival, some people apply colours to their skins and stick patches to their faces and necks. During her lecturership, she notices all the wigs and a girl called Mensha cries and cries to learn to use knives and forks. Later when she visits her native place to see her relatives during the vacation, people then surround her and enquire about new cars, and its coconut shell doors and fridges and refrigerators. At the beauty contest, she notices all the wigs, except one. For this alien cultural trend her 'brothers' protest and express their anger at the end.

The protagonist, Sissie tries to uphold her racial and social integrity by disdaining the national craze for European wigs. She still suffers from a sense of isolation, particularly since the Ghanaian 'brother's who have encouraged her in her militant African womanliness are still comfortable, and indefinitely, settled in Europe as perpetual students, with their European girl friends.

There are people and institutions who have been methodically degrading the native culture of African Countries. Many other people in the educational institutions imitate and follow the foreign culture. Thus the feeling that alien culture is superior to the native is prevalent not only in the middle class people but also in the lower class people.

The young university teacher, Sissie represents the fading as well as the resisting force of native culture and life of people in the post-colonial phase. In fact "She knew them as intimately as the hems of her dresses."[2] She feels pity when they dream of westernized practices in the life as superior one. Simultaneously she encourages the people if they never "try to struggle to look like white girls. Not strangling one's hair. And above all, not to wear the wig." (1)

Sissie detests the idea of wig-wearing, as it doesn't have any significance in the life. She opines: "Extremists are sure they are made from the hairs of dead white folk" (1) and considers wigs as "wig-made from peoples unwanted hair." (2) Sissie dislikes the unhealthy trend of wearing wigs. People who have to think about several other problems are blindly swayed away by aping the west. It pains Sissie who feels "perhaps her people had really missed the boat of original thinking after all." (2)

Though Sissie condemns the practice initially, she protests when some of her co-students express their anger against it. She asks them "But what was wearing wigs got to do with the revolution?" (2) Then her male friends reply thus "A lot sister. . . . Because it means that we have no confidence in ourselves." (2)

Thus the foreign culture misguided the people to look down upon their own native way of life and made them follow blindly the westernized life. Contrary to this trend, Sissy strongly believes that "she had always known that in her society men and women had more important things to do than to fight each other in the mind. It was not in school that she had learnt this." (2) Thus she advocates the people to put aside the bickerings on petty issues and to start thinking about their future life and national problems. It is the testing time for the people to know about Africa, and their gorgeous cultural life.

Another feature of postcolonial era is that people who came into power and pseudo-intellectuals in the higher academic institutions have tried to subvert the revolutionary character of the masses. They have been trying to redirect the everyday life of native masses again in the direction of western culture. Thus they have made the people not the think and work in a constructive manner. The culture which emerged in the process impressed the people strongly with its hypocritical charm. Sissie observes: "what was more, if they really wanted to see a revolution, why didn't they work constructively in other ways for it?" (2) Thus the charm of alien culture make the people lethargic and sidetrack their consciousness from serious to the senseless practices.

Ironically the 'brothers' and intellectuals are not free from the flaws. They are not prepared to face the realities and give up those aspects of their personal dreams which stand between them and their meaningful actions they aught to take up.

After the completion of her education in the university, Sissie visits some of the African countries where she does not find great change in the public life. Many people consider the imitation of foreign culture as an approach to new civilization. She is astonished to notice the 'wig-wearing' ranging from the air- stewardesses to the grade three typists in the offices. some of them have cut their hair discreetly short. Most of them have masses of flowing curls falling on their shoulders. Besides this the other girls and women whom she knew and remembered have turned their black smooth skin in to light skin. They did not do it uniformly. People are fond of looking like either Europeans or Americans. this imitation by the blacks stirs the agony and anger of Sissie. This rampant practice is spreading like a dreadful plague in the African countries. Sissie observes bitterly "A plague—that made funny patch works of faces and necks." (4)

After the vacation, Sissie comes to the national university as an Economics lecturer. As she prepares lectures on nations building for few weeks, she decides to tell them what was that. Unlike her student days, when Sissie encounters the students in her first class, it is a great surprise for her to notice the aged persons with their artificial wigs on heads. She thinks herself "who were these girls? Where had they come from to confront her with their youth." (5) Because they are older than her. They are like frightened lost creatures from villages and developing slums who come to the citadel of alien culture to be turned into ladies and to follow the alien cultural mores.

Then she notices all the wigs on the campus. "All the girls were wearing them. The biggest ones she had seen so far." (5) It irritates Sissie and she doesn't feel to stand and bear the killing influence of dreadful westernised imitation. A great anger and hatred spring out of her heart and Sissie "felt very hot and she who hardly ever sweated, realized that not only were her hands wet, but also streams of water were pouring from the nape of her neck down her spine." (5)

At this pathetic moment Sissie recalls the voice and concern of 'brothers.' They express their strong opposition to this alien 'wig-wearing' practice at the cost of their enriched way of life. When Sissie starts to express her dislike for the unhealthy practice of wig-wearing, the students think that something is wrong with the new lecturer. And they never try to think and look back at their past history and pleasant way of life.

In the end Sissie pays a visit to her native place to see her relatives during the vacation. There she happened to pay an unexpected visit to a national beauty contest. When the contest begins, all the contestants wear wigs except one. It is a painful and loathsome experience. She finds the whole experience so nauseating that "she hurried home and into the bathroom where she vomited—and cried and cried and vomited for what seemed to her to be days." (7) Sissie's staunch longing for native lifestyle, flavour, tradition and customs seem to perish at the hands of the blacks themselves.

It is not only the wig-wearing culture which predominantly exist in the African countries. The people of the villages consider the expensive things and articles as the symbols of real status and prestige. The pervasive impact of neo-colonialism introduced the culture of 'westernised world' and implanted the seeds of new false values to root out the simplicity of life.

When Sissie comes to her native place people do not enquire her about academic achievements and her contribution towards the welfare of the people. The questions they ask her are so painful that she cannot find answers for them. They surround her and ask "what car are you bringing home, Sissie? . . . And oh, we hope you brought a refrigerator. Because you simply can not find one here these days. And if you do, it costs so much . . ." (6) Thus people find themselves in the strong clutches of the westernised culture in the postcolonial African countries.

From the above analysis it clearly emerges that Aidoo quite displeased and disillusioned with the native itellectuals who in a way act as agents of the hostile alien forces. The reasons for this trend are firstly, there are some pseudo-intellectuals and politicians who have been developing a craze for "high-life songs." These people "scramble to pay exorbitant prices for second hand clothes from America." (1) The other reason Aidoo believes that there are "second rate experts giving first class dangerous advice. Or expressing uselessly fifth rate opinions." (1) Secondly, the 'brothers' who condemn the culture of wig-wearing, ultimately take up the hands of European girl friends and settle happily in European countries.

At the end of the story, Aidoo gives a sarcastic note on the struggle of a few pseudo-intellectuals who want to safeguard the native culture and lifestyle from the threats of the western culture. These intellectuals pose to preserve their native culture. They wish to reverse the influence and impact of the western culture on their lives without a strong commitment. They come out of their chamelion colours only in their everyday life. Instead of remaining the living examples of Africa native pseudo-intellectuals retreat from their countries to pursue the western education and culture just to remain the examples of alien agents only. Aidoo concludes: "But rarely all of them were abroad. In Europe, America or some place else. They used to tell her that found the thought of returning home frightening. They would be frustrated. Others were still studying for one or two more degrees. A masters here. A Doctorate there. . . . That was the other thing about the revolution." (7)

Thus Aidoo in "Everything Counts" aptly picturises the indirect influence and impact of western culture, which has unprooted the native culture from the lives of people under the postcolonial rule.

NOTES

1. Interview by Maxine Mc Gregor, *African Writers Talking*, ed. Dennis Duerden and Pieterse Cosmo (London: Heinemann, 1978), p . 18.
2. Ama Ata Aidoo, "Everything Counts," *No Sweetness Here* (London: Longman 1970), p. 1.

"To Read Her is to Discover Africa's Realities": Nadine Gordimer

K. VENKATA REDDY

Nadine Gordimer, the recipient of Nobel Prize for literature for 1991, is an outstanding contemporary writer of fiction in South Africa. Born in 1923 to a Jewish couple, she started writing when she was just nine. She has produced so far ten novels and two hundred short stories. She is less overtly political and more concerned with the human results of apartheid than the contemporary writers of fiction in South Africa. In all her writing she emphasizes feelings rather than making political arguments. Her writings sensitively explore the psychological and emotional consequences of apartheid. It is Turgenev she most brings to mind. She considers Nelson Mandela and Oliver Tombo as her leaders.

Among the ten novels Nadine Gordimer has produced so far, *A Guest of Honour, The Conservationist, The Late Bourgeois World, Burger's Daughter* and *July's People* stand out for their fictional excellence. *A Guest of Honour* is a novel of total immersions—physical, moral, social and political. It teems with human life, with landscapes of the map and of the mind, with events and insights. It is about an English colonial administrator, James Bray, who was expelled from a central African nation for siding with its black nationalist leaders. He is invited back ten years later to join in the country's independence celebrations. As he witnesses the factionalism and violence, that erupt as revolutionary ideals are subverted by ambition and greed, Bray is ironically forced once again to choose sides, a choice that becomes both his triumph and undoing. It is "a magnificent literary feat." The novelist has woven an intricate tapestry whose threads are love, friendship, idealism, freedom and betrayal.

The Conservationist is considered Gordimer's masterpiece. The beauty and largeness of South Africa is drawn with a breadth and scope that is breathtaking. It is a novel of enormous power. It presents a fascinating portrait of a man both reckless and calculating, left only with the possibility of self-preservation. It is about a white rich man, Mehring, who has all the privileges and possessions that South Africa can offer, but makes the life tragic. His wife, son and mistress leave him. His foreman and workers become increasingly indifferent to his stewardship. His farm is also destroyed by drought and floods. Isolated, at once cold and passionate, he challenges history in his determination that nothing shall change his way of life. Thus *The Conservationist* is a subtle and detailed study of the forces and relationships that seethe in South Africa today. As Paul Bailey points out, *The Conservationist* is "one of those rare works of literature that command special respect reserved for artistic daring and fulfilled ambition." The novel is a triumph of style too. The sounds, smells and foliage, the weaving lights of the veld are evoked in the passages of "cool delicate prose" that makes the author one of the ablest descriptive writers alive.

The Late Bourgeois World is a remarkable novel dealing with the crises which beset white people in the struggle against apartheid in the South Africa of sixties. Prescient, tender, pitiless and incisive, it reveals a great novelist at the height of her powers. It presents the tragic story of Max who has drowned himself. He wanted to live well with his wife, Liz Van Den Sandt, in the most honorable sense, but that was not made possible. Highly strong, sensitive and intelligent, he found it increasingly impossible to bear the burden of betrayal and the slow erosion of his self-respect. *The New York Times*, considered this novel simply "superb."

A novel of social and political import, *Burger's Daughter* is a riveting history of South Africa. It unfolds the story of a young woman's slowly evolving identity in the turbulent, political environment of the present-day South Africa. It presents a penetrating portrait of a courageous woman, Rosa Burger, whose father's death in prison leaves her alone to explore the intricacies of what it actually means to be Burger's daughter. Moving through an overwhelming flood of sensuously described memories, Rosa arrives at last at a fresh understanding of her life. Nadine Gordimer's subtle and fastidiously crafted prose sweeps this engrossing narrative to a triumphant conclusion. In the words of Joyce Carol Oates, the novel is "an intensely subjective prose-poem, mesmerising in the subtle cadences of its language." It is a beautifully manipulated work of art with its controlled density, subtlety and vitality.

A brave and imaginative work of art, *July's People*, is said to be "the best novel that Miss Gordimer has ever written" (Alan Paton in the

Saturday Review). It is so flawlessly written that "every one of its events seems chillingly, ominously possible" (*The New York Times,* Book Review). It is a brilliant and most artistic recordation of how two enlightened, liberal whites—Bam and Maureen Smales—are rescued from the terror of war by their servant, July, who leads them to refuge in his native village. The shifts in character and relationships give us an unforgettable look into the terrifying, tacit understandings between the black and the white. It gives us glimpses into a chasm of hatred and misunderstanding. Thus, *July's People* is an adventurous, powerful and despairing work. Like Jane Austen, Nadine Gordimer seems to aim at perfection in this novel and succeeds in her attempt. As a critic puts it, "every sentence she writes has the special impress of a true novelist's imagination."

Nadine Gordimer seems to be at her best in the short story. She has to her credit several volumes of short stories, the chief among them being *No Place Like, Six Feet of the Country, Livingstone's Companions* and *A Solidier's Embrace.* She is one of the finest practitioners of the short-story form in South Africa. When her *Selected Stories* was published in 1976, Graham Greene called it "a magnificent collection worthy of all homage."

In *No Place Like*, a collection of thirty one stories, Gordimer displays all her descriptive power and acute insight, "pinning Africa to the page like a butterfly for our inspection." To read these dazzlingly rich and impressively solid stories in their chronological order is to absorb, what has been happening in South Africa over the years. *Six Feet of the Country* comprises seven stories that distill the essence of what has been happening in South Africa in recent years, though people and landscapes so intensely and evocatively drawn.

In the sixteen short stories which constitute *Livingstone's Companions* Gordimer deftly evokes the Africa of today, where up-country and its town still reverberates. These stories are poised over the dilemmas of Africa and its denizens of both shades. Gordimer's incomparably precise, witty, unwhiny observations are webbed here with genius. The originality of these short stories is timeless. This volume of short stories is said to be Gordimer's "best work."

A Soldier's Embrace demonstrates once more that Nadine Gordimer is one of the most accomplished writers now working in English. The volume is "extraordinary not only for her style but also for her moral concern." In this masterful new group of stories, she continues to explore the physical and emotional landscapes of South Africa, through powerful themes that know no geographic boundaries.

Thus, both in her novels and short stories, Nadine Gordimer tells us of the strange and immensely moving peril of being a woman in South Africa, as well as the strange and immensely moving peril of the races. She writes:

> It is axiomatic that the urban theme contains the classic crises—tribal and traditional values against Western values, peasant modes of life against the modes of an industrial proletariat, and, above all, the quotidian humiliations of a black man's world made to a white man's specification. (*The Black Interpreters,* 55)

Nevertheless, Gordimer is more interested in people, and what makes them happy and unhappy, than in political moralities. She comes to us essentially as a fictional artist, achieving a harmonious fusion of her social and artistic concerns.

Like the nineteenth century novelists, Gordimer unites vast scope with minute attention to the ordinary. Her setting is Africa, but in her Africa we find ourselves. It is to the moments of greatest stress, when frail structures of idealism are being tested by shaking realities, that Gordimer gives the form of literature—novel or short story.

As a white novelist in black South Africa, Gordimer has a message to offer. She says:

> I do not fear the Blacks, but many whites do. My message to the self-appointed guardians of our culture is: There can be no such thing as South African Literature if it excludes Black Literature. (*The Black Interpreters*)

Rarely do we come across a white writer so deeply committed to Black Literature in South Africa. Indeed, 'to read her is to discover Africa's realities.'

Fictionalization of Reality: A Study of Nadine Gordimer's Art

SHOBHA SHINDE

Literature has often been used as a vehicle to express a country's political, cultural and emotional attitudes. Most African literature is an expression of its country's social change. The writers are concerned with the past and the present history of their country and this concern is reflected in their works. The social change that Africa has been subjected to since the colonization of the country, the cultural, political and missionary influences and its present state of independence with a growing awareness of both national identity and modern problems, find expression in most African fiction.

Milan Kundera in *The Unbearable Lightness of Being* (1984) observes, "The novel is not the author's confession, it is an investigation of human life in the trap the world has become." The African novelist attempts to translate his vision of ideal society into reality and the hardships he faces in carrying out this great task. The incorporation of unfamiliar anthropological material, fictionalization of nationalist and political aspirations and the recent trend of treating social and existential problems in artistic terms have lent a complex character to African writing.

Awarded the Nobel Prize for literature in 1991, Nadine Gordimer occupies a prominent place among white South African writers. She belongs to the group of white academics and radical South African historians who feel it necessary to realign South Africa nearer to place experience. Her basic thematic concern is the exploration of the interdependence of the blacks and whites keeping aside deep-rooted racial prejudices.

Nadine Gordimer, explaining her function as a writer, has stated that she has no alliance to South Africa "as a writer" but "as a person." She says: "I have no religion, no political dogma—only plenty of doubts about everything except my conviction that the colour bar is wrong and utterly indefensible. Thus I have found the basis of a moral code that is valid for me. Reason and emotion meet in it and perhaps this is as near to faith as I shall ever get."[1]

In her many novels like *Burger's Daughter, July's People, My Son's Story* and *A Sport of Nature*, Nadine Gordimer endeavours to create a portrait of reality that is human and has not been finalized in history. In recreating the freedom struggle of South Africa as a background to her novels, she skilfully blends history, politics and fiction with a prophetic vision. Gordimer distills political events into personal pain, which resonates through her writing. With an imaginative integration of private and public experience, she commits herself in *The Essential Gesture* "to describe a situation so truthfully that the reader can no longer evade it."[2] The South African freedom struggle against white dominion and apartheid has formed the subject of the epic saga of human suffering in Gordimer's *A Sport of Nature*, which could well be considered her masterpiece.

The title of the novel *A Sport of Nature* is explained in the epigraph as "Lusus Naturae a plant, animal etc., which exhibits abnormal variation or a departure from parent stock or type . . . a spontaneous mutation; a new variety produced in this way." Hillela is Nadine Gordimer's "sport of nature," a spontaneous mutation, a new type of untainted person. She is seductive and intuitively gifted for life. The novel is the bold sweeping story of Hillela's rise from obscurity to an unpredictable and unprecedented political power.

Hillela's mother Ruthie was all the colonial bourgeois illusions rolled into one. She hated South Africa and abandoned her infant daughter to the care of her two sisters. With sensitivity and understanding, Nadine Gordimer traces Hillela's growth through childhood and adolescence to the growing awareness of her own powers of seductivity. The emotional tensions in the family in which Hillela grows up and the social and political implications of the events around her, sharpen her perception of life. "In the newspapers were photographs of blacks burning their passes, raising fists and thumbs, staring elated defiance. Photographs . . . close black dots of newsprint cohered into the shout as it left an open mouth and the death kick of bullets that flung bodies into a last gesture of life."[3] In school, every morning during prayer time, Hillela and her cousin Carole offered thanks for the infinite mercy of God, in whose name other children were given an inferior education, were banished with their mothers to barren reserves, and deprived of fathers, forced to become migratory labourers in order that the children might not starve.

Forced to leave home because of an incestuous relationship with her cousin, Hillela secured different jobs as an assistant to a psychiatrist, in an advertising agency. Throughout the narrative we find interspersed hints of the heights to which Hillela will rise later in life. Changes in her personal life run parallel to the various steps being taken by the blacks against the white regime. Her social conscience is awakened again and again by the reports of police torture, beatings, electric shocks, extended denial of sleep to the black activists. Through the events around her Hillela arrives at an understanding of self. She leaves the country as a political refugee. The pretty girl is foot-loose. The ruptured kinships and displaced marginal emotions make her an exile. She finds herself in the middle of the African cause. Her personality flowers and blooms in the household of an embassy official. It is here that she picks up much that makes her assurance so provocatively perfect. She learns protocol, the range of safe subjects for conversations, the permissible limits of response. "Hers was the real, not the fairy story of Cinderella and her sisters; from a penniless, deserted girl, whose refugee status no one would vouch for—she had passed to the guest bedroom of an ambassadorial residence. There was no need to return ever." (201)

Hillela's marriage to a black South African revolutionary, Whaila Kgomani, make her a part of the political and historical movement of her country. She is one of the people who have given up being white. Along side her black husband, she negotiates with foreign countries for support to the African cause. "To the blacks, the unity of Africa was not another 'ism,' it was the dignity in brotherhood they had found at last in a world that had always denied them any other." To the English, the union between a black and a white became a symbolic assurance that they too, could be given absolution for their country's past. Hillela was an embodiment of the black political and ethical credo, non-racial unity against the oppression of a race. She oozed the animated confidence that she was escorting the first generation that would go home to freedom." (215)

Personal grief in the assassination of her husband acts as a catalyst for Hillela's political development, leading her into a heroic role in the overthrow of apartheid. Through the use of italics, Nadine Gordimer passes from prose into sheer poetry. "Grief is a rot, it belongs with the dead, but tragedy is a sign that the struggle must go on." (230) Hillela becomes an active partner of General Reuel, who leads an army coup in his country. The General gives her an African name—"Chiemaka Hillela, which means God has done well." The narrative shifts once again to the police atrocities and brutalities against the blacks.

The last words of Nadine Gordimer in the novel have become prophetic: "Hillela watched the flag as it flared wide in the wind, the flag of Whaila's country." On 10 May 1993, thousands of black South Africans danced to the tune of their national anthem as Nelson Mandela became the first black President of South Africa. *The Sport of Nature* is richly detailed and visionary, blending fact with fiction. It is a brilliant reflection of a world that exists and an affirmation of faith in one that has been born. Through the travails and tribulations of Hillela's life, Nadine Gordimer has exposed with exquisite accuracy the complicated nervous system of her country.

Gordimer's *My Son's Story* (1990) is a novel of conviction—a passionate novel. It is a tough unsentimental work of art which is moving in the extreme. It tells us about a school boy who plays truant and bumps into his revered father coming out of a cinema, with a white woman. An ordinary mishap, but the father is no ordinary man, and the family threatened by the affair, is no ordinary family. This highly intimate drama of personal conflict and public struggle is about love between a man and two women, between father and son and the vision of the freedom of a country. The central characters, Sonny, the teacher, his white mistress Hannah and his son Will are beautifully drawn and sustained in the progress of their individual confusion and suffering.

Besides the novel form, Nadine Gordimer has always felt comfortable with the form of the short story. *Jump and Other Stories* examines South Africa's interweaving of the political and personal. She offers here an orchestra of strange narrative voices—a child refugee fleeing from war in Mozambique; a black activist's deserted wife waiting for better times; a white farmer responding to the death of his illegitimate black son. Nadine Gordimer says, "A short story occurs, in the imaginative sense. To write one is to try to express from a situation in the exterior or interior world the life-giving drop, sweat, tear, semen, saliva—that will spread an intensity of the page, burn a hole in it."

In this collection of short stories a reader embarks on a journey across cultures—from the war in Mozambique to the beaches of South Africa, from the affluent suburb of Johannesburg to the back streets of London, over political territories from the underground to revolution. The settings of many stories are South African but the voices are different—the carefree teenager falls innocently in love with a terrorist, as in

The Sport of Nature. Jump is about the rites of passage into manhood by parachute and betrayal:

> "Of course it was war. . . ."
> "So?"
> "War isn't pretty. There is brutality on both sides. I had to understand. Tried to. But planes carried what I thought were refugee children to be saved from the fighting. The girls of twelve or thirteen, terrified they had to be pulled apart from each other to get them to walk. They were brought in for the men who were receiving their military training, men who have been without women, to satisfy them."[4]

This ordinary white boy, son of colonial middle class parents who had wanted him to be an accountant, who had joined the parachute club, becomes a betrayer of the cause of the blacks who have taken over the country. He stands at the window of his five star hotel room: "And now he is exposed. There is the bright stare of the beggared city, city turned inside out, No shelter here for life, the old man propped against empty facades to die. . . . The orphaned children . . . the men without ears and women with a stump where there was an arm. . . . Jump. . . . The stunning blow of the earth . . . the parachute sinking silken. He stands and then backs into the room. Not now, not yet." (20)

The Essential Gesture is a collection of Gordimer's many nonfictional pieces in which she has adopted the form of the essay. It has been called the story of an artist's awakening to literature, to Africa and to the great ugly reality of apartheid. The title is taken from Barthes: "A writer's work is his essential gesture as a social being." According to Gordimer, in South Africa, a double demand is placed on the writer. The writer's essential gesture, as a social being involves taking risks.

The South African writer's essential gesture, by which he enters the brotherhood of man, is the revolutionary gesture. Gordimer recognizes the society's right to make demands on the writer, even as she considers it equal to that of the writer's commitment to his artistic union.

If society has a right to make demands on the writer, the writer also has a right to affirm his allegiance to his art. She coins a strikingly paradoxical phrase: "To gain his freedom the writer must give up his freedom. The white writer's task is to raise the threshold of the consciousness of the white people as a cultural worker." The questions which *The Essential Gesture* raises are "should a writer be only a writer" or should he be "more than a writer." These questions generate an unresolvable conflict. A writer's integrity as a human being and a writer is in direct proportion to his ability to balance the conflict and bring about harmony.

Instances can be cited where the double demand that Gordimer refers to, far from generating conflict, acts as a catalyst to achieve some particular ends. Vaclav Havel, the famous Czech playwright, was the pioneer of the political movement in his country. He became the Czech president and the philosopher king. "His is a rare instance of a writer whose commitment to his people and to his writing is seen and shown to be one." Gordimer concludes, "The transformation of experience remains the writer's essential gesture; the lifting out of a limited category, something that reveals its full meaning and signification only when the writer's imagination has expended it."

NOTES

1. Kenneth Parker, *The South African Novel in English* (London: Macmillan, 1978), p. 115.
2. Nadine Gordimer, *The Essential Gesture* (New York: Penguin, 1989).
3. Nadine Gordimer, *A Sport of Nature* (New York: Penguin, 1987), p. 70.
4. Nadine Gordimer, *Jump and Other Stories* (U.S.A: Penguin, 1991), p. 16.

The Dilemma of a South-African White in Nadine Gordimer's *The Conservationist*

SUREKHA DANGWAL

South African world consists of a literature of a tremendous significance but to the entry into the door which has recently been opened to the world. Couple of years back, South Africa entered a new era of independence and democracy. The era of legalised racial discrimination ended and a new era began in which South Africa is reborn as a free nation after nearly three hundred years and returned to the fold of the comity of civilized nations.

The end of racism was the realization of the dream of South Africans for equality. Now in the free nation the main task is to liberate the people from the bondage of poverty and discrimination and to build a society in which all South Africans, black and white, would be able to prosper. The political freedom of the blacks of South Africa through a peaceful electoral process is the most significant event in the annals of human history for self rule since the independence of India blazed a trail of departure of colonial powers from Asia and Africa. The case of South Africa is even more significant. Elsewhere on the continent, the formal colonial masters withdrew to Europe. But the whites of South Africa who gracefully accepted a democratic dispensation, knowing full well the consequences of being a minority community have earned the gratitude of all who value democracy.

Before any appreciation of South African literature, one should not forget its close ties with political, cultural and social incidents. At any stage in its development, it is directly or indirectly influenced by the political development. South African writers with their peculiar history of 'apartheid' and the consequent political, cultural and psychological situations gave birth to a pure protest literature, and a portrayal of the hostility between the world of the white man and that of the black. To some extent, this conflict has killed the soul of aestheticism. Keats's concept of 'Art for Art's sake' does not fit into the reality of South African literature. There is no possibility for "Art for Art's sake in a book," feels La Guma, "based upon the truth about apartheid."[1] Basically, the white writers in South Africa are sympathetic to their fellow whites and talk of their dilemma in an alien land. They realize that their very whiteness signifies their alienation from black Africa. In the mind of a western man "a sense of loss" is very strong "under a white skin."[2]

On the other hand, the black writers are attacking the whites. The literature of South Africa is nothing but a "conflict between the white conquerors and conquered black, between white masters and black servants, between the village and the city."[3]

The country's history has been one of wars and perennial migration. Under the pressure of apartheid laws, the uprooting and replanting of Africans were the common phenomena of black literature. This has destroyed the cultural roots of South Africa and it is "out of culture," feels Gordimer, "from which man's inner being is enriched."[4] These are large forces at work in South Africa, of a sort that make individuals feel handicapped. A writer knows best and writes best about his immediate milieu. A writer cannot go beyond the potential of his own experience. Under the pressure of apartheid, the writer's potential feels hampered in South Africa. The black writers are totally ignorant of white man's experiences in his alien land, and the same applies to a white man and his understanding, sympathy and consideration of the black man's experiences of his native land ruled by the whites. "Each in turn finds himself shut out," and Gordimer accepted it as a "mutual loss of them as writers."[5]

The white writers of South Africa who are internationally known are Jack Cope, Dan Jacobson, Olive Schreiner, Doris Lessing and Nadine Gordimer. When these writers refer to black protagonist, they do so as outsiders with an even more limited knowledge of the native's everyday experience than the black writers have. But because of the political pressure, no fiction of any real quality has been written since the sixties by the black writer. They are between "the fear of expression and the need to give expression."[6]

Nadine Gordimer has described herself as a "romantic struggling with reality."[7] And it is Gordimer the romantic who is aware of western man's longing to soil beyond the ambit of his own world, beyond his conscious identity, in search of a vital centre, a primal wholeness and vigour, within the limits of Africa i.e. within his own psyche. As a white liberal, Gordimer has always found herself an outsider in her country. In her *The Late Bourgeois World* which was banned in South Africa, and got Nobel Prize in 1991, she has attacked apartheid. Gordimer knows that any form of slavery degrades the oppressor as well as the oppressed. "It would be uncritical to study the works of Africans and non-Africans," says she, "without reference to each other and neither group has a monopoly on the truth."[8]

In Gordimer's fiction, her white characters are questing for their individual identity and their Western-European selves as well. They are luckless Europeans who found only graves, not gain and glory in Africa. They are taking a self-preservative flight into Exile and Isolation. In one of her novels, *Occasion for Loving*, Jasse Stilwell insists on seeing herself as "intact alone."[9] James Bray, the Englishman, in *A Guest of Honour*, returns to Africa to set up a modern educational system in the country, "fades away behind the insect-stained wind-shield of the car carrying him to a violent death."[10]

The Conservationist, published in 1974, the Booker prize winner novel is the romantic longing of Mehring, a practical man of business, for his identity in the land of blacks. His sexual partner Antonia, an anti-government political activist, self-exiled in England to avoid arrest, laughs at Mehring's idea of being buried on his farm in his purchased soil. His idea of preserving his identity after death is futile because Antonia predicts, that the native will take back the land from Mehring's children and "no one'll remember where he is buried."[11] Antonia mocks upon Mehring's futile hope of insuring the survival of his name by passing the farm on to his son, "the four hundred acres isn't going to be handed down to your kids, and your children's children." (177)

The novel is about the black African past having signs of Europeans and their culture. For blacks the land is a symbol of hope and the promise of rebirth. But it is a "graveyard," a "cold thick hand" for Mehring. (141-42) He wants to plant trees that probably will not take roots in African soil. It seems to be omens of the approaching end of the white man's history in the continent.

The whites are enjoying life in South Africa only because of the labour and hard work of the blacks. Antonia pointing with her toe at a flower, she is in search of wholeness and regeneration. The flower is "a perfect mandala" and a "symbol of the universe." (174-75) Despite her quest of universal brotherhood and harmony, Gordimer's characters are also governed by the South African feelings of a separation from whites. Antonia does not identify any 'connection' between her body and Mehring's ego. After making love "it was always necessary to her ego to establish the difference, the vast gap between herself and a man like him." (106) To her it seems to be "bridged itself in pleasure." (106) This feeling of separation is a clarion call for whites to quit the continent. Mehring, the businessman, boss and seducer, is the most insecure person among blacks. His sense of security is under pressure and forces him to "sell the place."

The symbol of "egg" is used frequently in Gordimer's fiction. In *The Soft Voice of the Serpent,* a teen-age girl is quite disturbed about her future and loss of childhood. It takes a depressing form of "egg-smeared dishes into the sink"[12] of her married sister. And in another story in the same volume, a disloyal housewife tries to cope with the fear of her husband, "triggered by a kiss from her husband's egg-flecked mouth." (34) *The Conservationist* starts with "pale freckled eggs." It is a symobl of regeneration for both whites and blacks. "The eggs are arranged like marbles" and it is a hope for both "eggs and children." (9) Mehring likes the 'egg' that can break and run, like the "guinea fowl eggs," (11) held by the black farm children.

Mehring wants to protect the 'egg' or his masculine dominance from time's effect. He stands naked before the "calendar with a picture of a white woman without clothes." (64) He wants unbreakable eggs and Antonia is his ideal as she does not come under the spell of wine. He appreciates her, "a funny thing, the simple pretty ones disintegrate when they drink, the clever handsome ones become more beautiful, their sex comes to the surface." (72) Antonia, "shone, on wine; not the way a woman has a shiny nose," but like one of those "satiny stone eggs, striped brown agate that come from the desert back," (72) where Mehring was a child. It symbolizes the hope for whites in Africa. Mehring claims his possession and wishes to pass on to his later generations of white lords of the African land, fails when at last he thinks that "guinea fowl eggs will never hatch." (249) The indefinable girl's remark to him as a "pig iron" businessman is cracking like an egg into his ear and he feels the impressions of African soil deep into his heart.

Nadine Gordimer's developing consciousness of history through her novels contributes to a history of the consciousness of South Africa in the last four decades. Each of her novels is related to the cultural and social moment from which it emerges, and from which it, in turn, offers an inside perspective. However, despite such self-reflectiveness in her fictional mode, it is Gordimer's 'split historical situation' that accounts for a deeper history of South Africa. Many have been only too aware of her paradoxical social situation i.e., a white living in privilege, yet writing for the cause of deprived blacks. Though the ideological implications of her worth are populist, yet the modes of expression are elitist. She is unable to project a black future in anything other than 'resurrection' of the black corpse in *The Conservationist*. In South Africa death is a "final bankruptcy"[13] for whites and symbolic of a belief that the European has no future in Africa. Gordimer's prophetic vision has an end and finally South Africans are living in harmony with equal opportunities for whites and blacks. The power is in the hands of blacks. And the independence of South Africa is a realization for a white man that he "must lose himself in order to find himself."[14]

NOTES

1. Harish Narang and Gurleena Mehta, *Apartheid in Fiction* (New Delhi: Commonwealth Publishers), p. 4.
2. Nadine Gordimer, *A World of Strangers* (New York: Simon and Schuster, 1958), p. 31.
3. Lewis Nkosi, *Tasks and Masks: Themes and Styles of African Literature* (Longman, 1981), p. 76.
4. G.D. Killam, ed., *African Writers on African Writing* (London: Heinemann, 1973), p. 36.
5. Nadine Gordimer, "The Novel and the Nation in South Africa," in G.D. Killam.
6. Nadine Gordimer, "Writers in South Africa: The New Black Poets," *Exile and Tradition—Studies in African and Caribbean Literature* (Rowland Smith, Longman, 1976).
7. Nadine Gordimer, "A Writer in South Africa," *The London Magazine*, 5, No. 2, 1965, p. 28.
8. J.A. Ramsaran, *New Approaches to African Literature* (Ibadan: Ibadan University Press, 1965), p. 35.
9. Nadine Gordimer, *Occasion for Loving* (New York: Viking, 1963), pp. 7, 19.
10. Nadine Gordimer, *A Guest of Honour* (New York: Viking, 1970), pp. 423, 464.
11. Nadine Gordimer, *The Conservationist* (Middlesex: Penguin, 1978), p. 177.
12. Nadine Gordimer, *The Soft Voice of the Serpent* (London: Gollancz, 1953), p. 126.
13. Nadine Gordimer, *Six Feet of the Country: Fifteen Short Stories* (New York: Simon and Schuster, 1956), p. 9.
14. Nadine Gordimer, "The Novel and the Nation in South Africa," *Times Literary Supplement*, 11 August 1961, p. 521.

Is There a Moral in These Tales?[1] (And What Is It Then?): An Appraisal of Chinua Achebe as Novelist Teacher

P.D. TRIPATHI

> I can't endure the thought that a man of lofty mind and heart begins with the ideal of the Madonna and ends with the ideal of Sodom. What's still more awful is that a man with the ideal of Sodom in his soul does not renounce the ideal of the Madonna, and his heart may be on fire with that ideal, genuinely on fire, just as in his days of youth and innocence.[2]
>
> I just tried a topsy-turvy look at the world, because the upright view is so very gloomy. But it looks the same either way.[3]

Chinua Achebe is one of the two internationally best known Nigerian writers, Soyinka being the other one. Soyinka has won the Nobel Prize for Literature. He is by and large the writers's writer, an elitist, at least occasionally inaccessible to the common reader. Achebe instead combines the appeal of *taishubungaku* (literature for the masses) with the excellence of *junbungaku* (literature of quality), to use the Japanese expressions. He has a firm grip over popular imagination, in Nigeria and in Africa as a whole. He ranks with Senghor and Fanon, as Obumselu notes, in shaping the African sensibility.[4] An acknowledged craftsman, he assumes the role of a teacher. In his well-known essay on "The Novelist as Teacher" he says, "perhaps what I write is applied art as distinct from pure. But who cares?"[5] In view of his reputation, his hold on the African psyche, his skill as a writer and his pedagogic aesthetics, and evaluation of his teaching becomes necessary.

The search for a straightforward message in a creative work has its problems, from the plurivocality of language through the multi-layered semantics of literature to the historical determinants of meaning. But, as Jonathan Culler concedes, "in one sense, all projects involve interpretations."[6] It is indeed unavoidable and its prolematics are not as bizarre as might appear on a casual view. Paul B. Armstrong has convincingly argued the case for "limited pluralism" of interpretation with "criteria for validity" regulating "claims for legitimacy."[7]

Armstrong also formulates the notion of weak and strong disagreement.[8] In conditions of submerged (or is it suppressed?) tension as in the West,[9] ideological differences can possibly be ignored.[10] In the third world, where the potential of literature to educate or mislead is still reckoned high, acrimonious debate and exclusive claims, along political lines, over both literary cultural legacy and current production, is only too common.[11]

The present exercise is, frankly, an enquiry into the ethical and didactic rather than the structural. I briefly examine first a few stories from *Girls at War* (1972). I then go into an extensive scrutiny of *No Longer at Ease* (1960) with but a casual reference to other works.[12] Achebe, it appears, has but little to teach, advancing a regressive and despairing view of life. The paper suggests, by implication, the need for regular re-view of the finest (third-world) literary reputations.

I

In creative writing it may not be easy to make a decisive choice between moral/political options. In *The Rhythm of Violence* by the South African Lewis Nkosi,[13] for example, the act of sabotage planned by the multi-racial student group, though epitomizing popular resistance to discrimination and tyranny practised by the government, turns out to be self-defeating, as it finally hurts the non-racist young innocents. Violence surely offers no clear-cut choice.[14] But where the alternatives are matters of simple concern, the encoding of formulaic wisdom and its acceptance by the reader may not be less difficult.

For instance, the (apparently) most didactic story in *Girls at War*, that is, "Marriage is a Private Affair," is hardly as plain as the title suggests. Of more or less the same sub-genre as Maria Edgeworth's and Tolstoy's moral tales, and as good a piece as any of them, it fosters a double paradox. Its (surface) directness reduces its effectiveness as precept: some kind of indirectness is, I think, pedagogically desirable and efficient, for the capacity of a text to affect the reader's sensibility depends upon its ability to delight, cajole and convince.[15] The story, as if it were, turns upon itself in still another way. Nnaemeka, the Lagos-based son of Okeke from the countryside, marries, against his father's wish, the woman school-teacher of a different tribe. Eight years after marriage, Nene, the wife, appeals for her sons to be allowed to visit their grandfather. When the letter arrives, that night Okeke "hardly slept, from remorse—and a vague fear that he might die without making it up to [his children]."[16] Now, if marriage were a private affair in Nigeria and if Achebe knew no better, deep down, I do not see the point of the anticipated reconciliation as desired by both the young and the old. The story offers, I think, an example of community intervention in the creative process, confirming Achebe's view of the "mbari."[17] Unless irony is implied, the story should carry an amended title, "Marriage is NOT a Private Affair!"—The implication in either case, whether irony or no irony, is the same.

The sentimental glossing over with the reconstruction of a relationship gone awry, though it may be justified in one way or another, may not be the finest literary achievement. And in human life the complexity of personal relations can hardly be resolved by something to turn up a la Micawber. In the conflict between the old and the new, moreover, Achebe, even when he favours the young urbanized, is emotionally tethered to the past, incapable of breaking free.

He indeed endorses superstitious beliefs in "Dead Men's Path." Michael Obi, the young headmaster of a rural mission school, is committed to a high standard of teaching and to "modern methods." (70) As the rains come, the school, symbolically located in a well-enclosed area, is further separated, by beautiful "hibiscus and allamanda hedges in brilliant red and yellow," from "the rank neighbourhood bushes." Michael Obi then discovers the traces of "an almost misused path" across the school compound to "the bush on the other side." (72) He gets it closed and refuses to have it opened when the village priest informs him that it is used by the dead to leave the world, by the ancestors to visit their living relatives, and by "children coming in to be born." (73) When, soon after, a woman dies in childbirth, the school is overrun at night and extensive damage is done to the garden and the buildings. The white supervisor of the school comes for inspection and sends a report against Obi, spoiling his service records and the chance of (much-desired) promotion. The "indirect rule," said to have been practised by British imperialism, did not always, we may recall, permit a straightforward interference with settled beliefs and customs, though the missionaries and the mission schools were no doubt engaged in socio-cultural transformation.

Now, Achebe is critical here of the "misguided zeal" (74) of a young enthusiast, whose failure underlines the need for placating conservative sentiments. The choice of "Dead Men's Path" as the title of a previously untitled piece first published in 1953 (see Acknowledgement), perhaps metaphorically implies the futility of traditional beliefs—regardless of what happens on a particular occasion. But, if "misguided zeal" (—and where is the unorthodox action that cannot be so characterized is to blame for the failure it might entail, one wonders what course of action would be prescribed for the young couple in "Marriage is a Private Affair," if they had met with great parental opposition from the start: should they create extra reserves of moral and emotional strength to go ahead with the marriage, or had not they better keep clear of any "misguided zeal" and give in to customary pressure as Obi Okonkwo does in *No Longer at Ease* (who is, incidentally, Michael Obi like the school headmaster—28) to his own detriment and failure by not marrying the osu girl he was attached to?

In "Akueke," a girl's defiance of established mores is legitimized through the support of the maternal grandmother. In "Chike's School Days," where the child of the Christian union looks down "his nose at a free born" and refuses what he calls "heathen food" ("The white man had indeed accomplished many things" [36]),[18] Achebe also seems to approve of marriage with an osu. The story, first published in 1960, the same year as *No Longer at Ease*, is a slender piece where the osu theme is sketched in to be developed, as it were, in the novel. But Obi, of the longer work, is not misguided enough to marry an osu against his mother's wish. Achebe may find it difficult to recommend decisive action where the character is faced with critical oposition. Or is he, while claiming to be a novelist teacher, probing here the psychological, say under the influence of *Sons and Lovers*?

The psychological occupies significant space in "The Vengeful Creditor" (1971) which, I think, is the finest story in *Girls at War*. When free primary education is introduced, Veronica, the ten-year-old daughter of a poor widow, joins school; as this educational opportunity for children is soon after abolished, she has to leave school and is profoundly disappointed. She is then employed by the rich Emenikes, a working couple in the city, to look after their baby boy. She is told she will resume her studies when the boy grows up. She becomes impatient, for the child does not grow fast enough for her. So, to eliminate what she regards as an impediment in the way of her education, she gives him red ink to drink, hoping thereby to poison him. The story opens casually with Mrs. Emenike collecting grocery material at a supermarket. It ends with Veronica's mother calling upon gods to explain the abomination of attempted murder. The narrative skill, the sure and steady build-up to a crisis, the inventiveness, the unobtrusive flow of irony, the story can hardly be faulted in any way, technically superb. And yet, how do we explain Veronica's psychological (de)fault? It is surely free primary education, introduced without preparation, that first raises and then frustrates her ambition. Although he sides with the well-meaning but ineffectual Minister of Education, Achebe assigns all the logic, the eloquence, the rhetoric, the debating skill to the Minister of Finance who is against the system of free education and wants parents to pay for their children's education. (56-57) Achebe would no doubt prefer proper planning to bungled implementation, but this only strengthens the view that the introduction of free primary education, in the given context, was rash, precipitate. The "misguided zeal" of those who introduced it has caused but irreparable damage to an innocent child.

In what I say I assume the ever-present possibility of involuntary to deliberate over-reading and misreading, of reading one work into another, of reading both life and literature. But, whatever way we read him, Achebe's finest stories recommend a cautious approach and in no case advance any univocal thesis.

II

In our century of major historical shifts, social change as noticed within and through a family or a favoured region and community has been privileged globally in literature, with the chosen segment of humanity serving as the object, also the agent, of change, matters of partitive acquiring holistic significance.[19] Achebe has his contribution in this. *Things Fall Apart* (1958), *Arrow of God* (1964) and *No Longer at Ease* (1960) have been viewed, in this order, by Killam for example, as a trilogy. Through his (fictional) Umuofians, he creates a compiling awareness of the disintegration of Nigerian culture, though for him the white man has but a catalytic, peripheral role in the withering of the past.

The restitution of history is the point of *Things Fall Apart* and *Arrow of God*. "I would be quite satisfied," he says in *Morning Yet on Creation Day*, "if my novels [especially those that have been set in the past] did no more than teach my readers that their past—with all its imperfections—was not one long night of savagery from which the first Europeans acting on God's behalf delivered them." His use of Ibo proverbs is the stylistic authentication of an emotional attachment to history and its 'residual' elements. "I think," he says, as quoted by Killam,

> I am basically an ancestor-worshipper. . . . Not in the same sense as my grandfather would probably do it, you know, pouring palm-wine on the floor for the ancestors. . . . With me it takes the form of celebration and I feel a certain compulsion to do this. It's not because I think this will appeal to my readers, but because I feel this is something that has to be done before I move on to the contemporary scene. (59)

A celebration of the past, necessary for exorcising the haunting sense of European superiority, implies, paradoxicaly, an incapacity to celebrate the present or the future. As we shall see, Achebe's view of the contemporary scene reveals but uniform gloom, the bottomless pit of despondence.

No Longer at Ease is Achebe's first novel to deal with "the contemporary scene." Its protagonist, Obi, the grandson of Okonkwo from *Things Fall Apart* whose son, that is, Obi's father had become Christian, goes to England to study Law, comes home with an Honours degree in English and is appointed a senior civil servant under the British. The cost of his education abroad is met by the Umuofia Progressive Union, an association of working people committed to the development of their community.

Obi is an idealist of sorts. Not a snob like most people with even the smattering of modern education, he stays attached to his old friends, though without falling in with their cash-oriented expectations. He has an inflated sense of "the value of education," education "for service, not for white-collar jobs and comfortable salaries." (29) As a government officer, he could have wished to serve his country "well and truly," for the highly educated Nigerian does not have to depend upon corrupt means as the old men without "intellectual foundation." (17-18)

This idealist is finally hauled up for bribery. With his well-paid job, his education and idealism, he could be expected to avoid temptation. Everybody, including his friend Christopher, a graduate of the London School of Economics, favours corruption. He alone does not. But the reversal of character and conduct is predictable as narrative convention, and, given the over-all situation, his fall is hardly surprising. He confirms the fears of Mr. Green, his white superior in office, who kind of knew from the beginning (106) that something like this was going to happen. But the likely suspense of whether his idealism will turn into corruption and bribery is hardly important, for it is already resolved when the novel opens, in the court-room on the last day of the trial. The verdict itself is so immaterial we are never told what it was. Achebe is concerned with the cause and conditions of Obi's criminal act. The one remark in the court's summing up that is significant enough to be recorded is the observation of the judge, "I cannot comprehend how a young man of your education and brilliant promise could have done this" (2): it also appears to be the only thing in the courtly procedure that evokes a (pathetic) reaction in Obi.

The court-room scene cuts into the officers' club where, among compatriots, Mr. Green offers an explanation, "The African is corrupt through and through." The liberals of, say, the British Council may not accept this, but "over countless centuries the African has been the victim of the worst climate in the world and of every imaginable disease. Hardly his fault. But he has been sapped mentally and physically. We have brought him Western education. But what use is it to him?" (3) we go over to the Umuofians next and find that, so far as they are concerned, they feel unhappy as cheated, not by Obi's acceptance of money but because he is caught for merely twenty pounds! "I am against people reaping where they have not sown," says the Chairman of their Union. "But we have a saying that if you want to eat a toad you should look for a fat and juicy one."

The narrative goes back in time to explain why Obi did what he did. In a short paragraph at the end, Achebe returns to the beginning, as cyclicisation. "Everybody wondered why." The learned judge, the British Council man, the Umuofians, but nobody knew. "And we must presume that, in spite of his certitude, Mr. Green did not know either." (154) With Mr. Green appearing in the last sentence of the novel, we assume Achebe is countermanding the idea of climate and disease sapping the African character.

Achebe's can be construed into a four-fold explanation. In an ascending order, I first place accident. Unpredictable and irreversible, it may well queer the public and private pitch, in literature as in life. But, not necessarily a bolt from the blue, it may be the understandable consequence of events. If someone is accident-prone, moreover, fundamental personality traits may be at work. The theft of Clara's money which creates some serious problems can be regarded as a matter of chance. But it manifests a configuration of conditions as also the lack of care and caution in Obi's character: the possibility of a similar accident happening with Joseph or Christopher, Obi's friends, is remote, inconceivable.

Among the likely imponderable beyond human control, we may also reckon ancestral curse, inherited properties, Ibsen's ghosts. And that is number two, the second probable reason of Obi's degeneration. His predicament could be the extension of an old story, repetition with variation. He keeps away from his mother's funeral as his father had stayed away from Okonkwo's (125,145-46). The alienation of the younger from the older generation finds fulfilment in a widening gyre, an expanding spiral. But hereditary curse especially affects Obi's parents with little bearing on his own fall. Further, though Obi is seen to be his grandfather returned from the dead (49), he resembles him only in appearance, lacking his forebear's stature. Okonkwo acts in what he regards to be in the interest of the community as a whole, and his reparation leads to suicide. Obi, not abandoned or thrown away as Okonkwo was, does not command the same respect or admiration. Suicide for him is, moreover, the easy way out (36) that he would not go in for: the shedding of tears by him at the trial is in comparison but anti-climactic, incidental. Personal destiny as part of family history is thus in the present case but wayward, capricious, and the echoes of the past adduce but superficial similarity, though the past, we will see, has some relevance insofar as Obi's character is in some ways like that of his great-grandfather.

To go into the third likely explanation, social and financial pressure has a relatively meaningful role in what happens to Obi. He is surrounded by his bribe-taking fraternity, and has debts and family commitments. But the example of others he can ignore, and to meet the demands on him all he needs is proper management. Towards the end, with Mother and Clara gone out of his life, he could not care less whether or not he succumbs to temptation. But he is, like his great-grandfather, incapable of discipline, of economy, of looking after his interests. He also lacks the moral strength to act up to his ideas and ideals.

There's the rub, the fourth and I think the most important reason of Obi's fall. The fault lies in him, not in his stars or in social ethics. David Cook points to Obi's incapacity for normal man-woman relationship, the male egoist who cannot quite give himself.[21] Assuming the material burden becomes too great, Obi also fails to pay proper attention to his relationship with Clara. In a way his ego proves his undoing, the idealist with no grip of reality. But his vacillation more than his idealism, not his initial refusal to follow the precept and practice of his people and friends but his inability to sustain this that leads to his debacle.

Achebe then seems to argue that what might or might not be true of the Nigerian in general (Mr. Green's account) hardly explains an individual's conduct. "I am but a human being wearing a mask" (90), Obi once remarked: How do we know why anybody becomes sinful? We can only try to understand and excuse, with some kind of Christian forgiveness.

Yet Obi does not quite renounce his ideal, not deaf or dead to his conscience. "People say that one gets used to these things [acceptance of bribery], but he had not found it like that at all. Every incident had been a hundred times worse than the one before it." (153-54) He is the man of feeling who lacks the necessary finesse for action and achievement, the well-meaning individual who is wiling to bear the cross and bears it. Early in the novel, while explaining the nature of tragedy at the interview for his civil service job, he cites the example of a Christian convert from his village "who suffered one calamity after another" and said that "life was like a bowl of wormwood which one sips a little at a time world without end." (36)

True enough, but this defeats Achebe's "counter-discourse," his (apparent) project of repudiating the European view that the African is essentially, naturally, by nature corrupt. The issue is bypassed with Achebe advancing something like a law-court defense of extenuating social and psychological circumstances, or the Shakespearean view of an individual's character determining his destiny.

The pressure on other Nigerians may be similar to those on Obi. In this, he may be the Nigerian Everyman. But Achebe then endorses the notion that the typical Nigerian (read African), is, like Obi, incapable of thrift, foresight, "consecutive reasoning" (40), of "thinking of tomorrow." (87)[22] Abdul R. JanMohamed characterizes Mr. Green's explanation of Obi's "immorality" as "racial pathetic fallacy" in which "climate and disease account for moral degeneration." (158-59) Achebe has his own explanation. But neither dispensation, whether Green's or Achebe's, allows the possibility of escape. "Everybody said it was impossible to win" (80). Obi but proves the point.

The events of *No Longer at Ease* are set in late fifties when Nigeria was moving towards independence. Whether the country was competent enough or not for self-government was at the time a subject of common debate and discussion. "There is no single Nigerian," says Mr. Green, "who is prepared to forego a little privilege in the interests of his country. From your ministers down to your junior clerk. And you tell me you want to govern yourselves." (139) He is said to have resigned "when it was thought that Nigeria might become independent in 1956." (96) The event is delayed, but the subject of an honest and efficient indigenous civil service is still a priority item. On returning from Britain, the year is 1957, Obi notes, "with our great country on the threshold of independence, we need men who are prepared to serve her well and truly." (29)[23]

But his fall underlines the unsuitability of Nigeria for self-government. Aluko's *One Man, One Matchet* offers, instead, a relatively hopeful vision. Akpan, the protagonist, from the same historical period, has a less soiled and murky image. He compares well with the white expatriate, as modelled after him, and offers a viable alternative. He recommends a government of the local elite.[24] In this Obi may not be much different. He had written to Hitler as a boy (7) and justifies his action later. (33) He is for a "handful of men at the top. Or even one man with vision—an enlightened dictator." (40) Achebe has his reservations about such an approach and finds the Nigerian syndrome desperate, with its cycle of coup after coup from *A Man of the People* (1966) to *Anthills of the Savannah* (1988). In *No Longer at Ease* he no doubt offers an insight into how a person with a measure of idealism may have to give in to evil ways. But this only traces the course of personal deterioration. Between cognition and praxis in any case there is, at best, a huge gap, and the understanding that Achebe fosters leaves but little scope for action. Liberal (European?) humanism with its broad, hold-all sympathies and its rationalization of human weakness has surely its dangers and limitations, and can hardly be accepted as a matter of praxis and progress.

African writing occasionally perpetuates the notion of Africa as the dark continent, cultic and mysterious.[25] Achebe, maybe, generates some sunshine and clarity, if not what JanMohamed calls realism, an ambiguous and multi-valent term, as Jacobson notes.[26] But he is concerned with what I would call incidentals of biography, not with the underlying societal structures. Preoccupied with replying to the European paradigm, he operates largely within the framework of the colonizer's devising. Twice in *No Longer at Ease*, with reference to the British, he mentions bribery and corruption (translatable as greed and acquisitiveness), assigning a casual remark to an unreliable witness on one occasion (30) and quickly shying away from the idea on the other (40). On this issue, the western writer, in contrast, may not be partisan enough to exonerate the whites. E.M. Forster's Fielding, for example, on entering

India, bribes "a European ticket inspector" for a place on the train.[27]

Despite the reservations about the western discourse, then, Joyce Cary's Mr Johnson,[28] as it were, is of the unredeemable heart of darkness which, in opposition to Conrad's, cannot even claim as its own the outsider that strays in. In Achebe's fictional world, as in Joyce Cary's, the European is pure and remains immune to the local corrupting influence. Obviously the colonized cannot be absolved, or excused, by reference to the likely misdeeds of the colonizer. But can we bypass the impact of European presence in the third world, of dominance over dependence? To deny or ignore the material and spiritual influence of imperialist occupation promotes I think neither understanding nor action. For Achebe, the European has but a peripheral role in the predicament of his protagonists or his country and community.[29] The epigraph to *No Longer at Ease*

> We returned to our places, these Kingdoms,
> But no longer at ease here, in the old dispensation,
> With an alien people clutching their gods . . .

has but an empty resonance.

JanMohamed argues that Obi's understanding of the source of his inferiority sense permits him to free himself. Whatever this may mean, the idea of therapeutic release is by implication extendale to Achebe. But an epistemology of psycho-pathology offers at best a doubtful catharsis, of limited social value.

Whatever the cause and implications of Obi's fall, Achebe is wary of change and despairs of its possibility for the better.

In *No Longer at Ease*, some basic issues are enforced through recurrence. The foregrounding of corruption, with its (verbal) appearance in Obi's civil-service job interview (36-37) as well, is an example. The idea of the world being upside down (42), out of joints, is, similarly, never out of sight, concatenating with the pervasive but unobtrusive irony of Obi's name, Obiajulu, meaning "the mind at least is at rest." (6)

Among the recurrent preoccupations of the novel is the belief in destiny, in predetermination. After Obi's return from England, his old school friend Joseph recalls how this overseas journey had been prophesied long ago. (32) When Obi visits his parents after his return, Odogwu, the seniormost of the elders come to welcome him back, reminds everybody, "As it was in the beginning, is now and ever shall be, world without end." (47) In the course of three pages (47-49), he expresses the idea again and again, in almost the same words and, to confirm it, points to a similarity between Obi and his grandfather, assigning to the young man the greatness of his ancestor (49), which, as I see it, acquires an ironic amplitude in the text as a whole. At another stage in the novel, the President of the Umuofia Progressive Union says, "A man may go to England, become a lawyer or a doctor, but it does not change his blood. It is like a bird that flies off the earth and lands on an anthill. It is still on the ground." (146) Only a few pages later, Achebe notes in his authorial capacity,

> Beyond death there are no ideals and no humbug, only reality. The impatient idealist says, "Give me a place to stand and I shall move the earth." But such a place does not exist. We will have to stand on the earth itself and go with her at her pace. (151)

Miracles do not happen and the pace of the earth cannot be quickened. What else would a conservative manifesto say?

Despair and despondence, while questionable in itself, mark in the present instance a certain conformity with the European view that Nigerians (or Africans) are naturally corrupt, incapable of improvement. Achebe offers a rationalisation of what Obi does, but then Mr. Green himself blames the African climate, not the African people for the widespread corruption he views as characteristic of them.

The accent on despair, on the hopelessness of the human situation, especially in Nigeria, is more or less equally true of Achebe's fourth novel, *A Man of the People* (1966), the next novel to deal with "the contemporary scene." Achebe has, in theory, strong reservations about the "human condition" syndrome of modern European novel.[30] But he has, as Ben Obumselu shows, created in his protagonist Odili a character with all the anxiety and desperation, "the insecurities and frustrations and the fatal impairment of vision" that (existential) man is prey to. (19) The work offers no glimmer of hope. Max, the best of all the persons in the work, is morally as culpable as the other characters. He is different only in having inspired Eunice, his fiancee, to shoot his murderer in the chest "without asking to be paid." (149)

The reliance on a woman's loyalty (Odili himself finds comfort in Edna's devotion to him) as the only pleasant and helpful option brings Achebe disturbingly close to W.B. Yeats in his short poem on "Politics." Yeats records here a nostalgic preference for the fulfilment of youthful desire. With "the girl standing there," he cannot fix his attention "On Roman or on Russian/Or on Spanish politics." In spite of the "war's alarms," he wishes to be "young again" and hold her in his arms. The poem was written in 1938, only a year before the poet died, at the age of sixty-nine: he could I think have done precious little at the time for love or war or politics. In sharp contrast with this, Faiz Ahmad Faiz from the Indian sub-continent speaks, as an exemplary third-world voice, of other pains than those of love and other joys than those of sexual consummation.[31]

"Light breaks where no sun shines," as Dylan Thomas would say. Absolute despair, which we encounter again in *Anthills of the Savannah*, may be its own nemesis, cathartic and self-subversive (I read Lawrence Durrell for the first time when I was sick and depressed. I found him so depressing, I recovered!). But the authenticity of total glow is not enough, and we diligently look for and discover the silver lining. We draw comfort, for example, from the possibility of future birth suggested by the title and from the flower motif on the receding bus at the end of Armah's *The Beautyful Ones Are Not Yet Born*, a novel Achebe is sharply critical of for its unrelieved negativism.[32] The sense of loyalty Eunice felt for Max in *A Man of the People* could, similarly, be the symbolic straw we clutch at in a sea of despair. But the recourse to personal relations as ultimate, residual humanity clashes with Achebe's preferred choice of "applied art" and his notion of art as "mbari."

Achebe, we may recall, is authoritative and assertive in his critical works, theoretically profound and motivating. His creative works, again, highly readable and persuasive, comparable with major works from anywhere, make the appropriate literary appeal. Whatever his subject and setting, his is a competent treatment of the complexity of human situation. But what does he teach? What is the pedagogic objective to be assigned to his works? What are we meant to, and what can we learn from them, and how? What is the intention and objective of his teaching?

Despite the creative artist's mixed, complex sensibility and the multiple hermeneutic possibilities, literature and pedagogy I think cannot quite be viewed as separate, separable, unrelated disciplines. A literary work always offers, explicitly or implicitly, a perspective, motivating the reader with thought and feeling. Brecht's "alienation" surely implies no ideological non-commitment, at least on his part. As readers, in any case, we absorb not only the stylistic but also the thematic.

A "truthful," so to say realistic social account may have educational implications: if things are bad, we need to work hard for improvement. But what can we do if improvement is reckoned as impossible? "We will have to stand on the earth itself and go with her at her pace." Widespread Nigerian corruption is, as though, reality to be accepted uncritically—there must always be reasons for what the people do. And there is nothing we can do to improve the situation.

Achebe has doubtless upgraded Obi as a character, the Dostoevsky way (see the first quotation in the beginning of the essay), as "a man of lofty mind and heart [who] begins with the ideal of the Madonna and ends with the ideal of Sodom," though "in his soul [he] does not renounce the ideal of the Madonna," and "his heart [is] on fire with that ideal, genuinely on fire, just as in the days of youth and innocence." Obi, trapped under mental and social tension, may be deemed as representative of human psychology, of human life, from wherever.

But is that Achebe's goal and objective as teacher? Is he trying to emphasise the universality of human character with the existentialist view of life and literature that he is critical of? Whatever the over-all reality, then, it is permisible and justifiable for the Nigerian to go ahead and do what he does. He need not work for change and improvement, he cannot for it is impossible. In his creative writing, Achebe does not seem to have the same kind of theoretical single-mindedness as in his critical works.

The need for rigorous scepticism, for critical enquiry, for the refusal to accept a text at its face value, varies in direct proportion to its technical mastery, its capacity to influence people. But a refractory text, a text resistant to a specific interpretation, can be scrutinized for contrary implications and may be made to yield the agreeable moral similarly as a virtuous text, whether in the ethical or political sense. These reading strategies are pursued with diligence in the third world in particular, where political beliefs frankly affect literary appreciation. Reading is any way a purposive exercise, for ideological bearings enable the reader to meaningfully interact with a given text, instead of being passively dictated by it.[33] Deliberately divergent readings are, however, especially required for third-world literature: it is yet to be squeezed dry of interpretive options, and, where the printed word can cause political or moral mischief and benefit,[34] the possibility of text and author getting canonized, of their interpretation getting rutted has to be prevented.

The present article attempts a rebuttal of the myth around Achebe, the myth of the novelist teacher that may easily turn into the (involuntary) vehicle of a misleading notion of the nature of human predicament in the third world. In his novels and short stories, Achebe reduces the sociological to matters of individual psyche and personal destiny. Instead of suggesting any course of progress and development, he offers but a pessimistic approach, and views the Nigerian as inexorably trapped in an inescapable situation.

Which is all very well, and may be considered as truthful and realistic. But in the political uncertainties of Nigeria, where some years ago the ex-governor of a state was reported to have called upon the British to return to rule the country, a writer who claims to be socially committed, has to weigh the obvious to subtle nuances of his work. This is not to say that Achebe should have written a different novel, nor that he should have falsified his perceptions. But a book is the subject of open debate, not of sycophancy and unquestioning obeisance. In *Morning Yet on Creation Day*, Achebe has observed

> There are clear signs that critics and readers from those areas of the world where continuing incidents and recent memories of racism, colonialism and other forms of victimization exist will more and more demand to know from their writers just on whose ideological side they are playing. (12)

His readers and critics should be asking of him and he should be asking of himself, if, per chance and inadvertently, he has not been playing on the wrong side.

NOTES

1. The title of the article is modelled after Stanley Fish, *Is There a Text in This Class?* (Cambridge, Mass.: Harvard University Press, 1990). I also acknowledge a debt to Ben Obumselu, "Chinua Achebe's African Aesthetic: A Reconsideration of *A Man of the People*," though I disagreed with some of his formulations (see my response in *Ngoma*).
2. Fyodor Dostoevsky, *The Brothers Karamazov* (1879-80), trans. Constance Garnett (1912; William Heinemann: London, 1920), p. 110.
3. Ryunosuke Akutagawa, *Kappa* (1927), trans. Seiichi Shiojiri (1947; Tokyo: The Hokuseido Press, revised 1951), p. 86.
4. Ben Obumselu, "Chinua Achebe's African Aesthetic: A Reconsideration of *A Man of the People*," *English Teacher's Journal*, Lusaka, vol. 1, no. 2, Dec. 1977, p. 14.
5. Chinua Achebe, *Morning Yet on Creation Day* (London: Heinemann,

1977), p. 45.

6. Jonathan Culler, *The Pursuit of Signs: Semiotics, Literature, Deconstruction* (Ithaca: Cornell University Press, 1981), p. 16.

7. Paul B. Armstrong, "The Conflict of Interpretation and the Limits of Pluralism," *PMLA*, vol. 98, no. 3, May 1983, p. 341. I suppose we need to remember that language on its own may convey a variety of meanings even as the decontextualised, disembodied isolate of a class-room example, and that literature revels in paradox and ambiguity. What George Steiner calls "the historicity of speech acts," the "time-boundedness and mutations of . . . the most elemental of semantic modes" (p. x) further impede the deducing of a single or singular meaning. The interpretive act also depends upon social change and on individual taste and predilection: as Frank Kermode concludes from Shakespeare criticism over the centuries, a classic subsists in change, patient of interpretation (pp. 149-63, 164-80). In spite of all this, only a finite set of likely readings should be possible.

8. As Armstrong sees this, the difference, for example, between the structuralist and the Marxist exemplifies the strong variety of disagreement, while that between Marxists the weak variety (pp. 343-44). Weak or strong, disagreements have but ideological bases.

9. See Herbert Marcuse, "Representative Tolerance," in R.P. Wolff, Barrington More, Jr. and Herbert Marcuse, ed., *A Critique of Pure Tolerance* (Boston: Beacon Press, 1965).

10. It is not that controversial positions cannot be fostered by, or foisted on, the creative artist in the west. The ghost of Pound's fascism will long be haunting us. Witness also Gunter Grass, *The Plebeians Rehearse the Uprising: A German Tragedy* (1966), a sharp indictment of Bertolt Brecht. The introductory address by the author published with the play is anger uncontrolled, unqualified. But political and ideological differences in themselves and as the basis of literary approach and interpretation are rather widespread in the non-western world. See below, note 11.

11. In his Introduction to *Selected Poems of Pablo Neruda*, Louis Moguio reports "a matter of fashionable debate among Hispanic critics—a quarrel in which political sympathies and antipathies often play a more important role than literature." (p. 25)

12. Of Achebe's five novels, *Things Fall Apart* (1958: London: Heinemann, 1981), *No Longer at Ease* (1960; London: Heinemann, 1977), *Arrow of God* (London: Heinemann, 1964), *A Man of the People* (1966; London: Heinemann, 1977) and *Anthills of the Savannah* (London: Heinemann 1987), the second, third and fifth are concerned with the contemporary situation in Nigeria, while the first and third with the past of his Ibo community.

13. Lewis Nkosi, *The Rhythm of Violence* (London: OUP, 1964).

14. See Kenneth David Kaunda, *Kaunda on Violence*, ed. Collin M. Marris (London: Collins, 1980) and the first chapter of Frantz Fanon's *The Wretched of the Earth*, trans. Constance Farrington (New York: Grove Press, 1968, 35-95), "Concerning Violence." Against Fanon's sustained

advocacy of violence to oppose tyranny, Kaunda, though supporting the anti-apartheid struggle, has his reservations about the use of violence.

15. I do not see how literature and propaganda can be separated. The shouting of slogans is sometimes useful, but effective proselytizing needs a subtle approach, as that in literature. "Art as Propaganda," the sub-title of the chapter on "The Real and Social" in W.K. Wimsatt and Cleanth Brooks, *Literary Criticism: A Short History* (London: Routledge and Kegan Paul, 1970, vol. 3, *Romantic Criticism*), however, implies a biased view of the social and the real as a literary concern.
16. Chinua Achebe, *Girls at War* (1972; London: Heinemann 1980), p. 28.
17. For Achebe's view of the "mbari," see *Morning Yet on Creation Day*, pp. 21-24.
18. See *No Longer at Ease* (p. 53) for something similar from Obi's childhood. Obi's parents were pioneers of their day. Especially the mother, who, in her old age, just before her death, takes a rigid, inexplicable stand against Obi's marriage with an osu, was a rebel in her youth (pp. 150-51). In "Chike's School Days" as also in *No Longer at Ease* Achebe recreates his experience as the child of Christian parents. See Killam, p. 13.
19. There are several examples of this kind of literary concern. But *The Cherry Orchard* (1903) by the Russian Chekhov, *The Makioka Sisters* (1943-48) by the Japanese Tanizaki, *The Cairo Trilogy* (1956-57) by the Egyptian Naguib Mahfouz, *One Hundred Years of Solitude* (1967) by the Colombian Garcia Marquez can be cited as random examples from distant parts of the world.
20. G.D. Killam, *The Writings of Chinua Achebe* (1969; London: Heinemann, 1977), p. 60.
21. David Cook, *African Literature: A Critical View* (London: Longman, 1977), pp. 85-92.
22. When Achebe says on one occasion that Obi "was not really in the mood for consecutive reasoning. His mind was impatient to roam in a more pleasant landscape," (p. 40) one feels it is true of the character as a whole, and when Green speaks of the African's incapacity for "thinking about tomorrow," (p. 87) one recalls that Obi's great-grandfather from *Things Fall Apart* has the same problem, as a personal aberration though, for Obi's grandfather Okonkwo is a different type of character.
23. Nigeria became independent in 1960. Sir John Macpherson, appointed as Governor in 1948, was interested in Nigerianising the civil service. A Council of Ministers with local members was formed in 1951 as an advisory committee. In 1960, Lennox Body, the Colonial Secretary, talked of the lack of "trained staff." In the same year, Obafemi Awolowo, nationalist Yoruba leader, observed, "The defects in the British administration have turned to be a blessing in disguise. For, if British rule had been less inept than it was, the opportunity for Nigerians to demonstrate that they are qualified to manage their own affairs would have been correspondingly reduced." (See Schwarz, pp. 82, 101, 110, 116, 118-19 and Burns, Ch. XXV, pp. 285-90) While Aluko and Achebe give a clean chit to the

European civil servant, Awolowo does not.

24. See Shatto Arthur Gakwandi, *The Novel and Contemporary Experience in Africa* (London: Heinemann, 1977, p. 65) for his comments on Akpan's/Aluko's view that the educated Nigerians should form the local government.
25. Ayi Kwei Armah's *Two Thousand Seasons* (Nairobi: East African Publishing House, 1973), Camara Laye's *The Radiance of the King* (1965) and Yambo Ouologuem's *Bound to Violence* (1968), for example, offer no helpful image of Africa.
26. See Abdul R. JanMohamed, *Manichean Aesthetics: The Politics of Literature in Colonial Africa* (Amherst: University of Massachusetts Press, 1983), pp. 151-83, for a discussion of realism in Achebe's work. Also see Roman Jacobson "On Realism in Art" (1921; first published in Czech in Matejka, Ladislaw and Pomoraka, ed., *Readings in Russian Poetics: Formalist and Structuralist Views* [Cambridge, Mass.: The M.I.T. Press, 1971], pp. 38-46) for illuminating observations on what realism might or might not mean.
27. E.M. Forster, *A Passage to India* (1924; San Diego: Harcourt Brace Jovanovich, 1984), p. 61.
28. Joyce Cary, *Mr. Johnson* (1939; London: Michael Joseph, 1954).
29. Walter Schwarz in Nigeria (New York: Praeger, 1968), pp. 114-27, points out that the Nigerian attitude to Britain has, in general, been moderate. In the fifties, moreover, "West African opposition to colonialism became less bitter, and nationalist leaders became moderate in dealing with their British and French overlords." (See *West Africa Since 1800*, p. 280). It is understandable when Killam notes that the "colonial experience . . . created ambiguities" for Achebe, and "The political and economic possibilities afforded by the contact with the West are many and Achebe is optimistic about them." (p. 5)
30. See *Morning Yet on Creation Day*, pp. 24-25.
31. Yeats's poem is a well-known anthology piece. For Faiz Ahmad Faiz, see *Poems*, trans. V.G. Kiernan (London: Allen and Unwin, 1971), pp. 65-67. The original poem, in Urdu, comes from a collection first published in 1943.
32. See *Morning Yet on Creation Day*, pp. 25-27.
33. See Terry Eagleton, *Literary Theory: An Introduction* (Oxford: Basil Blackwell, 1983), pp. 79-88.
34. See T.M. Aluko in this connection. His Benjamin Benjamin in *One Man, One Matchet* "would be completely harmless in the London context. But it is an entirely different thing in [Nigeria] where the masses, illiterate and ignorant, believe everything that anyone that can read and write tells them." (London: Heinemann, 1964), p. 196.
35. Ayi Kwei Armah, *The Beautyful Ones Are Not Yet Born* (1968: London: Heinemann, 1984).
36 Alan Burns, *History of Nigeria* (6th ed., London: Allen and Unwin, 1963).
37. Frank Kermode, *Shakespeare, Spenser, Donne: Renaissance Essays* (New

York: Viking, 1971).
38. Luis Moguio, Introduction to *Selected Poems of Pablo Neruda*, ed. and trans. Ben Belitt (New York: Grove Press, 1963).
39. George Steiner, *Extraterritorial* (New York: Atheneum, 1976).
40. P.D. Tripathi, "Professor Obumselu on *A Man of the People:* 'European' Aesthetics?" *Ngoma,* Journal of the Dept of English, University of Zambia, Lusaka, vol. 1, no. 1, Jan.- June 1981, 1982.

The Neo-Anthropological Novels of Achebe

S.A. KHAYOOM

The voice of Africa in the world of letters tries to emancipate Africa from its literary stereotype. To the insider and outsider, Africa is no longer a gloomy phenomenon, a dark continent and a fantasy world. The novels of Chinua Achebe, the major exponent of the modern African novel, are a new way of looking at tradition to create a different order of reality through imagination. Achebe has subordinated the anthropology of his novels to the human condition. He is greatly concerned with the two realities of social man—his individuality and group identity, the legacy of colonialism, and the English language as the medium of expression of African experience and inspiration defining the relevance of colonial experience to the present. Achebe is the first Nigerian writer to transmute successfully the conventions of the 'novel' a European art form into African literature and to use 'African things' and employ certain native techniques of narration to give authenticity and African flavour to his novels in order to attract the native audience and overseas readers as well.

The first Igbo novel *Omenuko* (1933) of Peter Nwana was a biographical novel about an offence against the rural community and the consequent expiation and it being the novel by an Igbo, for the Igbo, about the Igbo, was an augury for the revival of vernacular literature among the Igbo. Achebe's novels, *Things Fall Apart* and *Arrow of God* in particular, are a study of Igbo tradition and are historical in perspective. Though Ekwensi's *People of the City* (1954) was the first modern Nigerian novel in English, in tone and essence a sophisticated and more lasting version of Onitsha literature, it is argued that the real tradition of Nigerian literature in English started with the emergence of *Things Fall Apart* as a typical Igbo novel to articulate social change through cultural conflict and tensions. When the early Nigerian prose fiction was dominated by Amos Tutuola's fantastic folklore romances and Cyprian Ekwensi's stories of city life, Achebe introduced psychological crisis into

Nigerian literature. Achebe delved deep into African tradition to write about Igbo life and culture from within as an Igbo.

African writing in English ought to be studied and its literary merit judged in the African context. The African novels by Africans about Africa from within a cultural, social and historical framework in a foreign medium face a linguistic problem and cultural crisis. The writer's use of artifices for imaginative purpose is handicapped by the lack of proficiency in the English language and its literary tradition and by the inadequacy of means of expression. Of course, the content of the novel in Africa is fully africanized by drawing on African oral traditions and the linguistic medium is used not merely as a means of articulation but to express African cultural experience to establish African authenticity. African novels of propaganda and awakening explore the quality of the contemporary African mind confronting outside forces and endeavour to project the distinct African personality. Most African novels are interpreted as extensions of social contradictions between 'culture' or 'symbolic order.' A majority of African novelists do not seem to be interested in writing 'Western' novels and in the subtleties of narrative technique and the literary designs—characterisation, motivation, depth-psychology and all the rest of it. The novel-in-depth, the pure novel of imagination is yet to emerge and flourish in Africa. Storytelling is the favourite form of narration for Africans. To the Western eye Amos Tutuola's books are 'amusing' and 'quaint.' But for Africans, Tutuola is undoubtedly a unique genius, albeit of declining power because of his incorrect English. Gerald Moore says, "Tutuola's books are far more like fascinating cul-de-sac than the beginning of anything directly useful to other writers. The cul-de-sac is full of wonders but is nevertheless a dead-end."[1] Tutuola has adapted the loose, episodic, non-sequential structure of the traditional tale to a novel format and his books are prose epics rather than novels. In the words of Dr. Parrinder, it is a beginning of a new type of Afro-English literature.

The novelist in Africa is an artist-historian and the cultural antenna of his society. He tries to counter the coloniser's derogatory remarks about 'raffia skirts' and help his people regain dignity and confidence in their traditional past.

The distinct feature of African novel as a third world novel, is the 'situational plot' where the importance of the central character is replaced by a group with similar experience and where the subject matter is not the individual's confrontation with his own problems but the confrontation of two divergent groups or cultures. Onuora Nzekwu's *Wand of Noble Wood* (1961) is a cultural document, highly informative like Achebe's two 'traditional' novels of Igbo culture in confrontation with the West. The protagonists in the novels of Achebe—Okonkwo, Obi, Ezeulu and Odili—present a people, a vision of life and a set of values and are products and victims of circumstances. And we are concerned with the fate of the community, and not the individual. Though the attention is focussed on one or two individuals in *Things Fall Apart* and *Arrow of God*, the story involves all the people, the entire community of Umuofia and Umuaro that forms the group consciousness of the novel. In the first novel, the entire community has experienced the debasement rather than one separate individual. Similarly the main characters in Ngugi's *A Grain of Wheat*, Raja Rao's *Kanthapura*, Aluko's *One Man One Matchet*, are the villages Thabai, Kanthapura and Ipaja respectively. Also in Soyinka's *The Interpreters* the reader's attention is drawn more to the 'situation' than to any particular individual by the novelist's multiple point of view technique. In this novel as in Ngugi's *A Grain of Wheat*, the main characters represent centres of concern contributing to the 'situation.' *The Interpreters* has no plot in the conventional sense of the term, "There is no orderly progression of events. The narrative has been given a form and pattern by the repetition of scenes and images which are used as leitmotifs."[2] Soyinka and Ngugi have also successfully employed the techniques of multiple flashback and a flashback within a flashback in their novels to focus the attention on the events that make the situation. In the African situation the individual, very often the protagonist, is at odds with his society. Okonkwo (*Things Fall Apart*), Waiyaki (*The River Between*) and Ntanya (*Dying in the Sun*) are some archetypal figures in African fiction contending with social forces. They are abnormal in their behaviour and unrepresentative as they mar the communal harmony and disrupt the close-knit social design by their eccentricity and challenging attitude. The isolation of the individual in the African novel makes him exceptional whereas the loneliness of the protagonist in the Western novel makes him typical representation of his society. The problem faced by the protagonist in the western novel is how to be in rapport with others and identify his problems with those of his society. But the central character in the African novel tries to assert his point of view without becoming a total outcast. Though there are certain disintegrating forces at work, it is the will of the majority that consciously contributes towards a coherent and organic African society. But the problem for the sensitive, self-conscious creative being is how to delink himself from his group and to assert his individuality. Obi (*No Longer at Ease*) and Samba Diallo in Cheikh Hamidou Kane's *L'aventure ambigue*, as men of two worlds experience similar tensions. Achebe is interested in rendering the African psyche in isolation. He switches from the simple situational genre of *Things Fall Apart* to the psychological novel where Obi, passive and confused, is in the foreground of the narrative.

Achebe's primary concern in the first three novels is more to capture a situation, telling about the central characters, than to make judgement. In *A Man of the People*, Achebe is exploring a new situation in a modern African state which is severing its ties with its traditional past. The isolated individual emerges in independent Nigeria confronting a new administrative set-up. Achebe does not merely conduct a sentimental journey into the traditional past but also explores the need to 'decolonize' it. Achebe's *Things Fall Apart* is an attempt to reconstruct in fictional terms a definition of African identity. Camara Laye's *The African Child* (*L'Enfant Noir*, 1953) is an autobiographical narrative of Laye's exile from his native culture and is about a process of deculturation. For many African writers like Achebe, Laye, Cheikh Hamidou Kane (Senegal) and William Conton (Sierra Leone), the essence of the explored African social reality lies in its symbolic nature. But Yambo Ouologuem has criticized this vision in his *Le devoir de violence* (1968), later translated into English by Ralph Manheim as *Bound to Violence* (1971), which is a reconstruction with brilliant philosophical implication of African history. While Achebe gives us a vision of culture conflict resulting in fragmentation of the organic pre-colonial society, we find a native leader emerging as the major victor in a power struggle in *Bound to Violence*. A change of vision of society has taken place—a movement from a nostalgic vision of African society to a Utopian vision of African fiction between Laye's *L'Enfant Noir* and Ayi Kwei Armah's *Two Thousand Seasons* (1973). Armah seems to evoke not the actual historical reality, but an African Utopia dominated by the alien forces of capitalism and imperialism. But South African fiction has served from its inception as a vehicle for expression of political aspirations. Ezekiel Mphahlele presents situations that are obviously political and drawn from the experiences. The African novel in general is viewed as distinct literary form in which basic social contradictions are reflected. The novel is characterized by the problematic hero unlike the epic hero who is non-problematic. Mostly, African novels are interpreted as extensions of social contradiction between 'culture' or 'symbolic order.' And most of the African novelists are not yet interested in the subtleties of narrative technique and the literary designs—characterization, motivation, depth-psychology and all the rest of it.

II

The situational novels of Achebe depend heavily on anthropological details to project the true traditional Igbo life and its cultural crisis. In *Things Fall Apart* Achebe has described the traditional Feast of the New Yam Year (chapter five), an occasion for Joy throughout Umuofia, a communal experience; we have the wrestling match (chapter six), a communal recreation; enthnological passages about the descent of the locusts and their harvesting by the villagers who roast and eat them as delicacies (chapter seven); the rituals of traditional marriage, gifts and the settlement of the bride-price (chapter eight); the birth of Ogbanje Ezinma and the search for Ezinma's iyi-uwa, her life spirit (chapter nine) and about the nine egwugwu that constitute the jury of the village and traditional trial (chapter ten). In the following chapters we hear of Chielo, the priestess of Agbala, the Oracle of the Hills and the caves and the traditional marriage followed by a traditional funeral (chapter thirteen). In *Arrow of God* also, Achebe devotes more than ten chapters out of a total of nineteen to the anthropological details about the Igbo life in Umuaro and Okperi. The ethnical content forms an integral part of the structure of the novels of Achebe and Ngugi but is less so with Cyprian Ekwensi. The anthropology of *Things Fall Apart* explains the cultural significance of Okonkwo's suicide: "It is an offence against the Earth, and a man who commits it will not be buried by his clansmen. His body is evil, and only strangers may touch it."[3]

Okonkwo's death dramatizes the spirit of Igbo life. It is the result of his unbending nature and hubris in confrontation with the demoralizing force of the new order. The anthropological background of the collapse of Okonkwo reflects the tragedy of the entire Igbo society as an apocalypse: traditional African society with all its glory and strengths is disintegrating simultaneously under the formidable external force of imperialism and the self-destructive impulses of the individual from within.

African fiction of the late 1950s and the early 1960s is anthropological rather than imaginative. Achebe's novels evoke the traditional life of the nineteenth and the early twentieth century. The famous wrestling match between Amalinze the Cat and Okonkwo (*Things Fall Apart*) must have taken place around 1875. The devastation and massacre at

Abame, the Whiteman's reprisal establishing his superiority in prowess as narrated to Okonkwo by Obierika, must have occurred in 1905. The report of the Secretary of the British colonial administration read by Tony Clarke, the junior Political Officer (*Arrow of God*) must have been the actual report of 1922 that dispensed with the policy of 'indirect rule' in Eastern Nigeria. Obi Okonkwo (*No Longer at Ease*) who represents the elite in Nigeria in particular and a generation in Africa, must have returned from England in 1956 to take up a job in the Civil Service though for a short period as recorded in the novel. The military Junta took over the civilian government in 1966 as prophesied and fashioned by Achebe in *A Man of the People* which appeared in print the same year. Anthropology represented by the Igbo traditional life in miniature and the traditional chief priest, Ezeulu as the incarnation of the values of Igbo society, is woven into the texture of *Arrow of God* to form part of the ironic design where the self-contained Igbo society is fragmented by the catalytic influence of the West, and the overweening chief priest. Also we find much parallelism between the social rites of Umuaro and of the Whiteman: "But we cannot come and go for nothing. When a masked spirit visits you, you have to appease its footprints with presents. The whiteman is the masked spirit of today."[4]

'Achebe country' cannot be strictly geographically defined. According to Robert M. Wren, it begins with the great Niger River below its confluence with the Benue. For Westerners it is Onitsha. It is Umuru, the great market city on the bank of the river. To the east of it about ten kilometers from the river is Ogidi, Achebe's father's town where Achebe was born. To the north, in about twenty-five kilometers, lies Awka, city of craftsmen in iron, and the native home of Achebe's mother and it is to Awka that Isaiah Okafor Achebe is sent for training to become a missionary of Church Missionary Society (Nwoye in *Things Fall Apart* and Oduche in *Arrow of God*). In the north of Ogidi is Obgunika where there is a cave believed to be the abode of a god, like Oracle of the Hills and Caves in *Things Fall Apart.* Awka's Oracle is called Agbala, the name Achebe gives to the Oracle at Umuofia. In *No Longer at Ease*, Achebe places Umuofia some fifty miles from Onitsha. Umuaro, identified with Umuchu, thirty miles south-west of Onitsha, is the union of six rival clans under Ulu (*Arrow of God*) in defence against Abame mercenaries. The fictional event narrated in the story of Abame of the killing of Dr. J.F. Stewart and the British reprisal might have occurred in a village in the south of Okigwe. 'Achebe country' is large enough to embrace the central province of Igbo-speaking people, a multitude of clans that share Igbo language, culture and tradition. The locale of *Things Fall Apart*, Umuofia which means 'children of the forest' (Ofia is 'bush,' uneducated, uncontaminated by European Urbanism), is symbolically named after the bushmen who inhabit it. It is argued that Achebe read Basden, an anthropologist who has become a legend in Africa and drew on his writings for details in the creation of his traditional novels. Achebe might have also read Leonard's *The Lower Niger and Its Tribes* about Igbos in particular and Africans in general where Leonard considered African fully human but with a tinge of 'barbarism' which he called 'a lower undeveloped phase of natural evolution' resulting not from racial inferiority but from a lack of 'opportunity to rise to the sublimer heights' of civilisation. Achebe's 'traditional' novels, like R.S. Rattray's *The Leopard Priestess* (1934), the first anthropological novel in West Africa about Ashanti social and oral tradition, openly didactic and hence less fascinating as a novel, are highly anthropological and descriptive of Igbo culture and history and have failed to attract the readers in certain quarters in the West. To the American reader, *Arrow of God* is but an ethnic reporting of ancient customs in conflict with new politics. Ronald Christ finds *Things Fall Apart* and *No Longer at Ease* 'long on native customs and idiom and short on narrative interest,' and he further says that the slender story-line in *Arrow of God* is soon lost in a plethora of local colour.

The strength of his novel *Anthills of the Savannah* lies primarily in Achebe's belief in story articulated through myth, legend, parable and folktale in the novel by the oldman of Abazon. The legend of Idemili, the daughter of the Almighty, in the novel reaffirms the intricate Igbo philosophy about rulers that in a pluralistic traditional system if one overreaches his authority, he is liable to severe punishment. And it is Idemili who ensures that moral law, peace and modesty would clothe authority. Sam, the dictator's "unquenchable thirst to sit in authority on his fellows," challenging Idemili's authority drives Sam to his disgraceful end. Ezeulu in *Arrow of God* is demented for his defiant transgression of the limits of his authority on Umuaro. By concluding *Anthills of the Savannah* with the voice of Elewa, a common person and a woman, representing Idemili's daughter, Achebe appears to have emphasized on the shift in values upholding Nigerian woman's growth and freedom from male domination, so powerfully expressed in *Things Fall Apart*, but in consonance with the 'core of reality' of Nigerian society.

The story of the tortoise and the leopard as narrated by the oldman of Abazon suggests the struggle of the people of Abazon against the repressive and tyrannical military regime of Kangan and inspires a section of the elite like Ikem to become conscious of their role and 'higher responsibility' in changing the set up and remoulding the society. *Anthills of the Savannah* subtly uses another oral narrative form, i.e., the prayer. The prayer recited by Elewa's uncle to bless Elewa's new born baby, is conventional and describes the power of God and welcomes the new arrival. But Elewa's uncle also adds new ideas in his prayer, "What happened to her father may it not happen again."

III

The Igbo traditional society as depicted by Achebe in the novels of 'African past' is masculine, hierarchal, self-contained, coherent and organic and in a curious way classical and above all, far from primitive. The society is governed by distinct social institutions and the legal system. And it manifests its authority in several ways. The will of the people that constitute the great assembly of Umuofia invokes traditional justice. Umuofia offers Mbaino the choice of war or a boy and a maiden as 'compensation' for murdering an Umuofian. Egwugwu, the masquerade council of ancestors and the ultimate tribunal, is another manifestation of the will of the clan. The trial scene in *Things Fall Apart* demonstrates the highly sophisticated, civilized social mechanism of Igbo society. Also the chief priest Ezeani enforces the will of the clan as the will of Ani, the Earth goddess when Okonkwo disrupts the peace of the peaceweek. The ndichie of high ranking elders is the decision-making body of the village. Agbala, the Oracle of the Hills and caves, also manifests the will of the clan. Anato Amalu (*Arrow of God*) consults the Oracle about the second burial of his deceased father, Ogbuefi Amalu. The Igbo 'tribe' is 'Presbyterian,' without rulers but run by a committee, often of elders and is achievement oriented. The 'Ozo' title of Igbo society has diffused the 'Kingship' and men of title become 'the hidden kings of non-royal clans' to constitute the decisive force of the community and are intermediary between the dead and the living and after death they find their place in mmo, the spirit world of ancestors. The Igbo 'tribe' is totemic; totem means 'brother-sister kin,' a visible symbol of unity, kinship, belongingness and common affinity. Every clan has an animal or part of it, a plant or a stone as its totem that is considered sacred. Royal python is considered sacred in Umuaro and Mbiano and is addressed as 'Our Father.' The Igbo society is polytheistic. Mother Earth, Amadiora, god of the thunderbolt, Idemili, the python god, Ogwugwu the giver and protector of life are smaller deities and Chukwu, the Originator and Sustainer is the High God whose will is too great to be known. 'Chi' is one's personal god and the guiding spirit and in some measure 'Chi' keeps civil order and the clan. Loyalty to self incorporates loyalty to kinsmen for what 'Chi' affirms, the clan affirms too. In the Igbo life, the male-female spiritual duality well expressed in the words of Achebe: "Wherever something stands . . . something else will stand beside it,"[5] pervades all 'things' and it becomes the central paradox of *Things Fall Apart*. As G.D. Killam puts it, "While continuing emphasis on male activities acquisition of wealth and wives, the production of children, courage and resourcefulness in sport and war—informs the surface interest of the novel, all activity in *Things Fall Apart* is judged by what is or is not acceptable to 'Ani, the Earth Goddness. . . .' In other words a powerful 'female principle' pervades the whole society of Umuofia."[6]

In the traditional society, Agbala, the Oracle of the Hills and caves, partly manifests the will of the clan and the male authority in Umuofia. But he is served by the priestess Chielo and there exists an undefined association between the deity and the priestess. Agbala is the voice of the Earth and is called 'Father,' the counterpart of the Earth, the great mother. In the Igbo masculine world, wife is ranked with other property as observed by Basden, wife is something more, as a member of the clan and has a 'place' and a 'share' in the clan. In *Things Fall Apart*, the first wife of Nwakibie is privileged to wear the anklet of the titles of her husband for the palm wine ceremony. Kinship, the powerful uniting force, essential to civil order in Igbo society is maintained by courtesy and ceremonies. The offering and breaking of Kola nut is a sign of goodwill and the personal emblem that the guest draws at the threshold with the lump of white clay given to him, is a mark of respect and friendship. 'Kola' is metaphorically used when Okonkwo tells Nwakibie 'I have brought you this little kola'—a pot of palm wine and cock to seek favour from him. Achebe's second novel *No Longer at Ease* is built around 'Kola' or bribery. A man approaches Obi, places same notes on the table and says: "This is Just—small Kola . . . we will make good friends."[7] The traditional feasts offered to the villagers at the three major marriage ceremonies—the settling of the bride-price, the Uri while sending their daughter to her in-laws after marriage and the Isa-ifi a ceremony marking the acceptance of the bride into her husband's family—strengthen their sense of belonging and through marriage the lifeblood of the clan is renewed.

In the novels of Achebe there is a shift from the communal life to the individual consciousness and back to the ethnic group. The individual is vulnerable in isolation and introspection but is reabsorbed into the mainstream of the community. Achebe tries to describe the symbolic order of African society from a culturalist point of view and as a detached observer he attempts to highlight the setbacks of traditional culture responsible for the social and political maladies of the modern Nigerian society with a sense of irony and satire. 'Okonkwo was afraid of being thought weak' is the central irony of his fall. In the second novel the ironic effect is due to the unique structural pattern of the novel. In *Arrow of God*, it is ironic that the religious head of the community, Ezeulu, indulges in secular logic while the elders of Umuaro suggest spiritual remedies. In *A Man of the People*, Chief Nanga is ironically called 'a man of the people.' In his 'traditional' novels, Achebe satirizes the attitude of the villagers and their personal animosity when deliberations take place at the market place. In *No Longer at Ease*, the hero is caricatured as anti-hero—a young graduate, fickle and feeble with disturbed conscience. Achebe in *A Man of the People*, his brilliant satirical farce, exposes the inadequacies and follies of his society and the cynical attitude of political opportunists to exploit their tradition for personal ends. As *A Man of the People* has exposed the social and political maladies of young Nigeria, *Anthills of the Savannah* too deals with the chicaneries of state administrators, other functionaries and the ruling elite in various capacities, also with 'issues of leadership,' offering a critique of contemporary Nigerian society and making writers like Ikeru became conscious of their 'higher responsibility' to 'correct the situation' and remould the society.

The success of *Anthills of the Savannah* is due to its supposedly post-modern literary qualities and its techniques which have their origin in the Nigerian oral narrative tradition. The novel depicts the life in Kangan, an imaginary African state, in the nineteen-eighties and attempts to re-establish proper relationship between the rulers and the ruled. Achebe appears in this novel to have upheld the Igbo truism—'no man ever won judgement against his clan,' rediscovered in national politics, that is responsible for the sticky end of Ezeulu in *Arrow of God* and for toppling of civilian government in *A Man of the People*. In *Anthills of the Savannah* president Sam is overthrown by the chief of staff in a coup and Chris is shot dead by a policeman.

Achebe tries to define African myths in terms of its relevance and meaning to contemporary living. He has refuted the concept of 'dark Africa' and Negro's socio-cultural inferiority as 'the unspoiled child of nature, the noble-savage-carefree, spontaneous and sexually uninhibited.' He has enlightened the outsider especially, that the tribal elders are wise men, repositories of ancestral wisdom, heroic explorers, giants of prodigious force and children not of darkness but of the Sun. Achebe also deals with a man of two worlds, a product of hybrid culture—another myth in his novels. He has drawn on oral literature to give authenticity and African flavour to his novels and has used flashback, a cinematic device, to put events and actions in significant order. His richly textured anthropological novel *Arrow of God*, published after *No Longer at Ease*, is a flashback to and consolidation of Achebe's first anthropological novel. In *No Longer at Ease*, the inevitability of Obi's fall is structured around a flashback. In *A Man of the People*, Odili, the narrator has detailed in a flashback how he hates and has opted out of politics. Achebe's characters are more a psychic case, dramatically caricatured as 'living theatres of social dilemma.' For some, *Things Fall Apart* is more a descriptive novel with no proper 'character growth.' But Achebe's characterization in the novel is in terms of action. He uses little dialogue and two or three brief passages of introspection to build up Okonkwo's heroic personality. But the reader is provided with enough information about Okonkwo and his virility. In *Arrow of God*, Ezeulu is characterized more by what he does rather than by description or lengthy authorial commentary. The character of Ezeulu is further developed by introspection, through dreams and conversation with himself. The unique aspect of Achebe's characterization is his frequent use of oral literary material-proverbs spoken as dialogue. Most of his characters are symbolic of the age, society and country.

Achebe's novels are not mere novels of values of life. He has carefully maintained the balance between the realistic portrayal of the human condition and values and the definite structure of the fable. His stories present a conflict between tradition and modernity, the social and the occult or within the Clan between the Community and the individual. Achebe has deftly interwoven the Igbo social customs into the fabric of his story and attempts to show from his ambivalent position the complexities of a colonial situation and decolonization. People who are disabled in the old tradition, like Okonkwo, Ezeulu, Obi and Odili, become the first victim in the new dispensation. Achebe doesn't consciously intrude himself into the narrative. The simple story of the novels of Achebe tells itself. Achebe's novels are a vehicle of self-discovery and try to define African identity and make the African re-discover his cultural roots. The four novels of Achebe are united by a common purpose revealed in the mode of narration. He has made two major innovations in his novels in an attempt to make then distinctly African. He has created and employed with great professional competence pidgin English with African colour to suit the narration and the characters involved in action and has devised the ways of presenting in fiction the wide range of Igbo rituals like Pumpkin Leaves Festival, New Yam Festival, the daily rituals of greeting and fare-well and the rites of second burial—embodying the values of traditional life.

Achebe as the sensitive point of his society, haunted by a sense of past, has in his novels registered his encounter with history and tries to restore the African character to its history. His characters maintain vital relationship with their social and economic landscape. The aspirations and the world view of the characters are shaped by a particular environment in a particular historical phase. The Okonkwos and the Ezeulus are the makers of history and lives in history. Achebe has bestowed on them human dignity and recreated the dynamic spirit of Igbo community. His novels are not mere fictionalized anthropology to be examined from a cultural point of view but are a work of art literally speaking. It is not the anthropological detail but the detail transformed into the social particular that is Achebe's distinctive contribution. In fact the whole trust of Achebe's Igbo quartet is to redeem the African novel from the anthropological cliches and present an ongoing living reality of the Igbo society. Achebe's 'traditional' novels—*Things Fall Apart* and *Arrow of God*—are not anthropological but historical novels. Achebe traces the decline and fall of the Igbo Utopia towards the political nightmare of a corrupt society and in this he renders meaningfully the Igbo encounter with historical change and crisis and uses creatively his sense of the pastness of the present and the presentness of the past. His novels are a 'new' kind of African fiction of the novelist and the anthropologist in Achebe. Adopting the structure and unity of a modern novel, Achebe could successfully and effectively create the African atmosphere strengthened by the oral performances. His sensitive use of language, his historical perspective and his memorable characterization have made Achebe a leading African novelist.

NOTES

1. Gerald Moore, *Seven African Writers* (Three Crowns, Oxford University

Press, 1962), p. 39.

2. Charles R. Larson, *The Emergence of African Fiction* (Macmillan, 1978), p. 29.
3. Chinua Achebe, *Things Fall Apart* (London: Heinemann Educational Books, 1958), p. 186.
4. Chinua Achebe, *Arrow of God* (London: Heinemann, 1964), p.190.
5. Chinua Achebe, *Morning Yet on Creation Day* (London: Heinemann, 1975), p. 99.
6. G.D. Killam, *The Novels of Chinua Achebe* (London: Heinemann Educational Books, 1969), pp. 19-20.
7. Chinua Achebe, *No Longer at Ease* (London: Heinemann Educational Books, 1960), p. 168.

The Influence of W.B. Yeats's *On Baile's Strand* on Chinua Achebe's *Things Fall Apart*

STEPHEN CRISWELL

The title of Chinua Achebe's first novel, *Things Fall Apart*, is taken from W.B. Yeats's poem, "The Second Coming." Many critics, such as Judith Gleason and A.G. Stock, have commented on the influence of Yeats's view of history and time (his notion of the cyclical nature of existence symbolized by his "gyres," or intertwining cones, illustrated in such poems as "The Double Vision of Michael Robartes," "The Phases of the Moon," and "The Second Coming") on Achebe's novel. However, Chinua Achebe may have found in the writings of W.B. Yeats more than merely a shared view of the rise and fall of civilizations (as A.G. Stock suggests); it is possible that Achebe was influenced by the way Yeats utilized Irish folklore to dramatize his interpretation of the historical process. Yeats found the legends of the Irish hero, Cuchulainn, to be an especially useful vehicle for his cosmological paradigm, and one such legend, "The Death of Aife's One Son," seems to have served as the inspiration for certain events in *Things Fall Apart*. Several parallels between the Irish legend and Achebe's novel suggest that the Nigerian novelist was inspired by the "The Death of Aife's One Son" and, more specifically, by Yeats's version of the legend.

"The Death of Aife's One Son," from the Ulster cycle of Irish myths, legends and tales, began as an orally-transmitted legend and was eventually recorded in the Yellow Book of Lecan (a fourteenth-century monastic manuscript) as one of the pre-tales, or *remscéla*, of the Irish Epic, the *Táin Bó Cuailnge*.[1] The legend recounts an episode in the life of the *Táin's* hero, Cúchulainn, who according to Ulster legends was trained in arms by Scáthach, the warrior queen of Alba (Scotland). While under Scathach's tutelage, Cúchulainn aids his teacher in defeating a rival warrior queen, Aife, whom Cúchulainn defeats in single combat. In exchange for her life, Aife agrees to bear Cúchulainn's child.

Cúchulainn returns to Ulster before the child is born, but before departing, he tells Aife to name the child Connla (or Conloach). He gives her a gold ring and tells her when the boy's finger has grown to fit the ring, she must send him to Ulster.

Years pass, and Aife receives word that Cúchulainn has married someone else. Jealous, Aife vows to get revenge through her and Cúchulainn's son. She sends Connla, who by now has grown into a young man and, like his father, possesses extraordinary strength and ability, to Ulster. Before Connla leaves, Aife gives him three commands: "The first never to give way to any living person, but to die sooner than be made turn back; the second, not ro refuse a challenge from the greatest champion alive, but to fight him at all risks, even if he [is] sure to lose his life; the third, not to tell anyone his name on any account, though he might be threatened with death of hiding it."[2]

When Connla arrives on Ulster's shore, the high-king, Conchubar, sends one warrior after another to intercept the boy and get his name. When he refuses to reveal his name, the boy is challenged to single combat by the warriors, each of whom Connla easily defeats. Finally, Cuchulainn, seeing that the young man should prove to be a worthy opponent, challenges Connla. The two warriors fight equally in strength and skill, but Cuchulainn eventually uses his secret weapon, the *gae bolga*, the terrible javelin that only Cuchulainn can use. The *gae bolga's* blow is fatal, but before the young man dies, he reveals his name and shows his father the gold ring that Cuchulainn had given to Aife. Cuchulainn becomes mad with rage and grief. Fearing that the crazed hero will turn on his fellow warriors, King Conchubar orders his druids to bewitch Cuchulainn into taking his rage out on the sea. The druids's spell takes hold of Cuchulainn, and he fights the waves for three days and nights until he is eventually exhausted.

W.B. Yeats retells this legend in his play, *On Baile's Strand* (1903), making several changes to the story in order to use the legend to dramatize his conception of history. In *A Vision*, which Yeats published in 1925, the poet outlines his complicated and at times mystical system of history. According to his system, history moves in cycles, or gyres, from objectivity (the "primary gyre") to subjectivity (the "antithetical gyre") and from subjectivity back to objectivity. The period of the subjective age emphasizes the individual, the heroic passion, worldly glory and human achievement; the objective age is marked by service to others, passivity, civil concerns, conformity and uniformity. When the objective age reaches its zenith and soon begins its decline, the subjective age begins its ascension, and vice-versa. As Yeats explains in *A Vision*: "Each age unwinds the thread another age has wound, and it amuses one to remember that before Phidias, and his westward-moving art, Persia fell, and that when full moon came round again, amid eastward-moving thought, and brought Byzantine glory, Rome fell; and that at the outset of our westward-moving Renaissance Byzantium fell; all things dying each other's life, living each other's death."[3] According to Yeats, as one civilization or age begins to fall (for example, the Greco-Roman period), an age or civilization with opposing or antithetical concerns (in this case, Christianity) begins to grow.

In *On Baile's Strand*, Yeats reworks the legend of "The Death of Aife's One Son" to illustrate the decline of one age—the subjective age, represented by the self-determined, physically powerful Cúchulainn—and the rise of another—the objective age, represented by the civic-minded leader of the society, King Conchubar. While the plot of Yeats's play superficially follows the ancient Irish legend, Yeats makes specific deliberate alterations to the story. In his version, the story opens with Conchubar's having called Cúchulainn to a meeting of the kings of Ireland. Conchubar convinces Cúchulainn to swear obedience to him and his state. In the growing objective age, the subjective hero is feared and distrusted and must be brought under civil control. Conchubar explains to Cúchulainn:

> Look at the door and what men gather there
> Old counselors that steer the land with me,
> And younger kings, the dancers and harp-players
> That follow in your tumults, and all of these
> Are held there by one anxiety.
> Will you be bound into obedience
> And so make this land safe for them and theirs?[4]

Cúchulainn yields to Conchubar's command, reflecting on the days when men "praised whatever life could make the pulse run quickly," and realizing "that's all over." (32) Cúchulainn understands that the gyre of the heroic age is winding down.

The first order that Conchubar gives Cúchulainn is to defeat the young man who has just arrived on Ulster's shore. As in the legend, Yeats's Cúchulainn does not know that the boy is his son, but he admires his strength and prowess. At first the hero refuses Conchubar's command, but his warrior's pride soon gets the better of him. He fights and kills the boy. When he soon discovers that he has killed his own son, he flies into a rage. But in Yeats's version it is unclear if Cúchulainn is tricked into attacking the waves, or if he chooses to do so, having no one else upon whom to exact his revenge. The play ends with the image of Cúchulainn foolishly but tragically, even heroically, fighting the sea, the "invulnerable tide"[5] which serves as a symbol of the endless process of change. It is this process, or cycle, that is the source of Cúchulainn's pain. Cúchulainn, in the ultimate heroic act, takes up arms against the eternal process that potentially makes all heroism meaningless. He cannot stop the rise of the objective age, but he can remain true to his heroic nature and stand against the process of change, though it means his defeat.

It is this tragic-heroic stand against change, along with the motif of infanticide, that most clearly links Yeats's play with Achebe's *Things Fall Apart*. Obviously, Achebe was inspired to some degree by Yeats, as "A Note about the Title" on the copyright page of the Fawcett-Crest edition of *Things Fall Apart* notes:

> The title . . . is taken from William Butler Yeats's poem, "The Second Coming," . . . As Judith Gleason points out in *This Africa*, the choice of titles reflects the author's awareness of debilitation that Okonkwo foresees in *Things Fall Apart*: "For *Things Fall Apart* comes from the world of Yeats's cataclysmic vision, and how the Irish poet would have appreciated the wild Old Nigerian."

If it is clear that in writing his first novel, Achebe had in mind Yeats's poem and the view of history which it dramatizes, then it is reasonable to assume that Achebe was familiar with and possibly inspired by Yeats's other works, particularly *On Baile's Strand*. Both works contain the key plot elements of the hero murdering his own son (or in the case of Okonkwo his foster-son) and the hero's final futile stand against inevitable change. While these motifs are by no means limited to these two stories, the pairings of the motifs and the theme which they both develop seem unique to these two works.

The first motif, the murder of the hero's son at the hands of the hero himself, plays itself out in *Things Fall Apart* somewhat differently than in Yeats's play; however, the contexts and results of the action are similar. Okonkwo does not kill his own son, Nwoye, but rather Ikemefuna, the hostage-child who becomes part of Okonkwo's family and, for all practical purposes, his foster-son. Achebe describes Ikemefuna's feelings for Okonkwo, stating. "He could hardly imagine that Okonkwo was not his real father."[6] Like Cúchulainn with his son, Okonkwo admires Ikemefuna's qualities and regrets having to kill him. Unfortunately the village has decided that the boy must die, and fearing that the community might think him weak, Okonkwo refuses not to participate in Ikemefuna's execution. Okonkwo, like Cúchulainn, is so driven by his pride that he willingly kills his own son. Though he is not driven mad, Okonkwo's participation in the killing seems to initiate his eventual downfall, culminating in his final actions—the killing of the messenger and his subsequent suicide—actions which could be perceived as insane, but which nevertheless have a tragic-heroic quality to them.

These final actions of the novel's protagonist closely parallel, thematically, the actions of Cúchulainn at the conclusion of *On Baile's Strand*. Okonkwo is faced with the collapse of his whole way of life. The arrival of the Christian missionaries signal the beginning of a new way of life contrary to Umuofia's traditions, and the British Raj which soon follows facilitates the destruction of Umuofia's old order. The process of change that Okonkwo faces is "incomprehensible, uncomprehending, invincible,"[7] and completely unsympathetic toward Okonkwo's old ways. The District Commissioner best represents not only the power of the British Empire, but also this indifference of the process of change; he tells Okonkwo and others in his community: "We shall not do you any harm . . . if only you agree to cooperate with us. We have brought a peaceful administration to you and your people so that you may be happy . . . in the dominion of our queen, the most powerful ruler in the world." (178) Okonkwo must choose between accepting this powerful new order or standing firmly, but perhaps futilely, against it. He chooses to fight though he realizes that the days of Umuofia's heroes are over. Like Cúchulainn, Okonkwo recalls the "days when men were men," but realizes "worthy men are no more." (184) He takes the only opportunity for action open to him and kills one of the "white man's" messengers. His actions seem unreasonable to the other villagers: "He heard voices asking: 'why did he do?'" The only response Okonkwo gives to their questions is to hang himself. However, Okonkwo's friend, Obierika, provides the answer, telling the British officials, "That man was one of the greatest men in Umuofia. You drove him to kill himself." (191) The source of Okonkwo's suffering and his seemingly incomprehensible actions lies in the coming of the British to Umuofia, or more accurately to the process of change their arrival represents. Like Yeats's Cúchulainn, Achebe's Okonkwo recognizes the inevitable end of his old way of life, but he chooses to act against the process of change and commit some act of self determination, even if his only choice is suicide.

Though it is unclear to what extent was influenced by Yeats's reworking of "The Death of Aife's One Son," the parallels between Achebe's novel and Yeats's play suggest that *Things Fall Apart* owes something to *On Baile's Strand* and its ancient Irish source. More importantly, however, examined together the novel and the play illuminate each other, bringing out in both the essential idea of the tragic-heroic stand against the inevitable eternal process of change.

NOTES

1. Thomas Kinsella, "Introduction," *The Tain*, trans. Thomas Kinsella (Oxford: Oxford University Press, 1969), p. x.
2. Lady Isabella Augusta Gregory, "Cuchulainn of Muirthemne: The Story of the Red Branch of Ulster," *A Treasury of Irish Myth, Legend, and Folklore*, ed. and comp. Claire Booss (New York: Avenel Books, 1986), p. 658.
3. W.B. Yeats, *A Vision* (New York: Collier Books, 1937), p. 271.
4. W.B. Yeats, *On Baile's Strand*, in *Eleven Plays of William Butler Yeats*, ed. A Norman Jeffares (New York: Collier, 1964), p. 29.
5. W.B. Yeats, "Cuchulainn's Fight with the Sea," *The Collected Poems of W.B. Yeats*, ed. Richard J. Finneran (New York: Collier Books, 1989), p. 36.
6. Chinua Achebe, *Things Fall Apart* (New York: Fawcett-Crest, 1959), p. 58.
7. A.G. Stock, "Yeats and Achebe," *The Journal of Commonwealth Literature*, July 1968, p. 109.

Name-Calling: Problems of Racism and Representation: Achebe and Conrad

TERRY COLLITS

This paper will revisit the moment when the great Nigerian English novelist Achebe called the great Polish English novelist Conrad a 'bloody racist.'[1] It will have in mind recent debates within postcolonial studies, around such names as Frantz Fanon, Homi Bhabha, Gayatri Spivak and Benita Parry, and over such questions as authenticity, representation and political efficacy of academic activity.[2] In a sketchy way, it will interrogate current conditions for employing the powerful received category of 'racism' in the critique of colonial and postcolonial texts.

Before doing all that, however, I will begin by attempting to identify myself. I am an eighth generation Australian, or more precisely in current Australian parlance an 'Anglo-Celtic Australian.' In my case, this hybrid label is reasonably accurate, but in relating me to the oldest type of Australianness (some believe, to *authentic* Australianness) it obscures a lot in Australian cultural history. My oldest known forebear was certainly English, transported to Botany Bay as a convict in 1803; but the dominant strain in my genealogy is Irish Catholic. In the 1940s, mainstream Australia was Protestant in name, but already secular, and the large Catholic minority was anything but secular: aggressively separatist, we attended our own schools to be taught religion by nuns, wore distinguishing uniforms, practised medieval religious ceremonies in Latin and ate fish on Fridays. For one such ceremony, at the age of six I was dressed in a white silk blouse and pantaloons with a silk purse full of rose petals around my neck, these to be kissed then floated before a processing statue of the Virgin Mary, as I slowly walked backwards down the church aisle. Inside the church this was fine; but outside, walking a mile along a public highway dressed in this garb, I felt distinctly different. Our difference was often expressed as a strong but ambivalent anti-Englishness, less rationally, in an attitude of being at once embattled and spiritually superior.

Of course, such an anecdote will hardly identify me or even define adequately my writing on the subject, though it may have an oblique relevance. What I hope it does do, partially, is underline the impossibility inherent in one of the most prominent elements of current postcolonial theory its necessary preoccupation with specifying the subject-positioning of the postcolonial cultural critic. The impossibility and the necessity of this new problem are that while 'imperialism' and 'racism' must go on meaning 'western imperialism' and 'white racism' in this context the ground on which the older oppositions rest (colonizer/colonized, centre/periphery, European/native) becomes increasingly more contestable. Are Rushdie or Achebe to be thought of as Third World writers or First World intellectuals or internationalist hybrids?[3] Gayatri Spivak's important question, "Can the Subaltern Speak?"[4] might be matched by another: 'Should the western postcolonialist academic stop speaking? Similarly, Benita Parry challenges poststructuralist colonialist analyzers such as Spivak herself or Homi Bhabha on the grounds of their deconstructionist practices denying the political potency of an earlier anticolonialist polemics. Parry herself has been charged in turn with a nostalgic hankering for the authentic native voice and impatience with Bhabha's celebration of the mimicry and hybridity of a recent postmodern, postcolonial writing,[5] but Parry could simply be read as looking for the lost political sharpness available to a Fanon in the 60s which she feels all but disappears in the subtleties of our current moment.

At the simplest level, one aspect of the task for the postcolonial critic, 'white' or 'black,' is to overcome the traditional bland tone of academic discourse, now that the objects of academic analysis (colonial and postcolonial texts) quite obviously relate to questions of human happiness and misery on a global scale. An older assumption of value-neutral objectivity as the sign of the academic must now be put in question in terms of the supposed innocence or transparency of the postcolonial analyst. Prior to this moment, the embarrassment of Achebe's tendentious attack on Conrad is partly that he argued a powerful and unexpected case, one which exposed a problem in Conrad's writing elided even in political analyses of his novels, just as the 'political' itself was all but forgotten by the academic criticism of Conrad for forty years after the author's death (years not untouched by ongoing European imperialism). A second source of embarrassment is that the attack was made in a manner that transgressed fundamental academic assumptions of politeness strategies of containment) at a moment when Western academics were not yet ready to deal with such a transgression (in the first instance, it was largely left to Third World intellectuals to thrash out the ensuing debate). Finally, one suspects, the embarrassment related to an uneasy sense that this blunt, cogent and passionate accusation of a racism embedded in the language of the great tradition of English fiction might just have a special validity: the authentic voice of protest coming from a highly respected, internationally acclaimed African writer.

Authentic or not, Achebe's challenge represents an ongoing problem area for First World intellectuals, either directly in the terms in which it was then cast—the subject of 'racism' became a discrete subset of cultural and literary studies through the 1980s[6] or in the current anxiety about what might constitute progressive political efficacy through interventions that remain, by and large, academic. To make it personal once again: in what terms do I, inhabiting an arguably European body and employed by an English department in a 'Western' university, correct Achebe's passionate misreading of *Heart of Darkness* without reinforcing what hardly needs reinforcing: the hegemony of Western discourse? and that especially if the necessary correction is made by an appeal to the second dominant strain of postcolonial theory today, the poststructuralist concern with the instability of the text and the relative insignificance of authorial control? For Achebe's error was not so much that he misread Conrad's attitude to blacks as that he took *Heart of Darkness* for a stable and unproblematic embodiment of its author's beliefs in the first place. And yet, if Conrad has produced in *Heart of Darkness* a text so slippery that it can never be pinned down, locked into the play of an inconclusive ironic meditation which leads no more to the need for political action than to a quietest awareness of the philosophical absurd, what has such a text to do with political change?[7] It is at least arguable that Conrad's description of the Belgian Congo, much later in his life, as "the vilest scramble for loot that ever disfigured the history of human conscience and geographical exploration"[8] has a sharper political edge than Marlow's narrative in *Heart of Darkness*.

Part of Achebe's charge is that the Africans in *Heart of Darkness* 'dehumanized' (denied that fuller human presence and individuality given the Europeans) not so much through mis-representation as under-representation. In Conrad's earlier colonial novels set around the Malay Archipelago, the 'native' characters received equal space as it were, with the Europeans. These novels—*Almayer's Folly, An Outcast of the Islands*, the second half of *Lord Jim*—avoid the problematics of representing non-European characters in an English novel largely by working within the available conventions of popular romantic and adventure fiction, enriched by personal observation of locales and Conrad's reading of anthropological and travel writings. They don't hesitate at all to introduce various Malay or Arab characters to English fiction. The greater sophistication of *Heart of Darkness* derives precisely from the text's very refusal to represent African life 'directly': what looks reductive to Achebe, reading this European's account of his own grandparents' generation of Africans, can be seen from a different perspective as a deep challenge to the old colonial novel's claim to cosmopolitan omniscience. Hence the limited, prejudice-ridden liberalism of the Marlow character-narrator. *Heart of Darkness* encloses within its own rigid limits the liberal-humanist ideology underpinning European imperialism at the end of the nineteenth century (the mission, the work ethic, the superiority of civilized man) and faces it with its inbuilt contradictions. To this extent, it can be read as an overcoming of colonial discourse, while appearing unable to imagine anything beyond the colonialist nexus but a limitless darkness (into which presumably Kurtz—though not Marlow or the reader—is permitted to peer).

In terms of literary history, Conrad's journey moves from the practices of traditional realism (which apparently came easily to him) to those more tortured texts which are seen as precursors of high modernism. The exact moment of cross-over is registered in a letter of Conrad as early as 1896, while he was struggling with *The Nigger of the "Narcissus"*:

> The more I go on the less confidence in myself I feel. There are days when I suspect myself of inability to put a sentence together, and other days when I am positively incapable to invent anything that could be put into a sentence. Gone are alas! those fine days of 'Alm. Folly' when I wrote with the serene audacity of an unsophisticated fool.[9]

The emphasis here, on a writing experience, is close to his later remarks about his own African experience in 1889: "Before the Congo I was just a mere animal."[10] The experience of growth in both instances is associated with well-nigh traumatic depression. My point is that this difference is not just a literary or personal phenomenon; it has political consequences.

Achebe is partly right: the consistent refusal of *Heart of Darkness* to represent 'fully' its non-Europeans (even to give them names) leaves the text open to the charge of making its Africans appear as less than human. But Conrad shows us the Congo at an early moment of colonialist intervention; he makes no attempt to include or even offer informed speculation about precolonialst Africa, prior to this 'fantastic invasion.' The story frames that moment of disruption at a fairly advanced stage, and meditates on its present and future implications. Within the context of ruling imperialist ideology, that inhabited by both the text and its contemporary readers, some of the instances which Achebe finds offensive can yield quite different meanings. This can demonstrate what I mean by calling the text slippery or unstable: Marlow's attitudes mimic European prejudice, as when he comments on the 'improved specimen' of a native who was his fireman: "to look at him was as edifying as seeing a dog in a parody of breeches and a feather hat walking on his hind legs. A few months of training had done for that really fine chap."[11] The racism of the contempt is only unsteadily balanced by the patronising sympathy. And yet even Marlow here is more concerned with the processes of historical change involved than with individuals as fixed entities. One message could be that Africans should stay in their place, as should Europeans too: the blacks belong in the dark jungle, Europeans have advanced beyond that state. By the same token, though, Marlow's confused stance undermines that very ideology of progress on which the European presence in Africa depends for justification. Again, if it is some sort of Darwinian progress that is implied, the evolution of the human species is not being furthered by the direct efforts of the more advanced race, whose use of the natives is here challenged, not on moral grounds, but in terms of wanton stupidity. Nor are such moments as these, which Achebe seizes on as instnaces of racial slighting, fixed in the text as final Marlovian truths. Within pages and in the least 'balanced' moment of the text—the native attack on the boat—Marlow's sanity and moral sense undergo a profound test with the death of the black helmsman. The disturbed, even schizophrenic, writing of this episode certainly privileges Marlow's experience of the event; but now the very inarticulateness of the native is transformed into a potent indictment of Europe:

> We two whites stood over him and his lustrous and inquiring glance enveloped us both. I declare it looked as though he would presently put to us some question in an understandable language, but he died without uttering a sound, without moving a limb, without twitching a muscle. Only in the very last moment as though in

> response to some sign we could not see, to some whisper we could not hear, he frowned heavily, and that frown gave to his black death-mask an inconceivably sombre, brooding and menacing expression.[12]

When pressed, few elements in the Conrad text fail to reveal such a duplicity (or hybridity, to use Homi Bhabha's important term). *Heart of Darkness* recalls the event in Conrad's own life-experience, his Congo journey of 1889, when he ceased being 'a mere animal' and entered into the 'higher' state of the bad conscience of the European intellectual at the moment of so-called 'high' imperialism. He moved from being a mere animal of a writer, I am suggesting, when he gave up the pretence of knowing the native. With whatever qualifications, I think this can be called a progressive move.

Achebe's own English novels about the early moment of European trespass into Africa, *Things Fall Apart* and *Arrow of God*, also employ tactics of hybridity and mimicry, rather than professing an authentic African experience. His representation of the master-narrative of European imperialism now marginalizes the European experience of that long process; the English reader must, in turn, stumble over a text clogged with untranslated Ibo words and untranslatable concepts, practices and assumptions, and be confronted by the harshest contradictions and cruelties of traditional Ibo village life presented with anthropological calm and without the salve of sympathy. The European interventions are shown as at once grotesquely ignorant and lethally effective.

This last of course is not light years away from Conrad, and in other respects Achebe's modern recreation of this historical period can be read as in dialogue with *Heart of Darkness*. The dialogical strategy of the novel, its use of pastiche, becomes explicit in the chapters which present the life of the British District Officer while at the same ;time mimicking the undisturbed flow of the old colonial novels:

> He would wonder that unspeakable rites went on in the forest at night, or was it the heart-beat of the African darkness? Then one night he was terrified when it suddenly occurred to him that no matter where he lay awake at night in Nigeria the beating of the drums came from the same elusive distance. Could it be that the throbbing came from his own heat-stricken brain? He attempted to smile it off but the skin on his face felt too tight. This dear old land of waking nightmares![13]

In many ways, Achebe's colonial novels do go beyond Conrad. But the conditions of publication within which he chooses to write in his own language, English, thereby reaching an international readership (and as editor of Heinemann's African Writers Series to take many of his countrymen with him) as well as the deep inscriptions of 'Westernness' which mark his own twentieth century subjectivity, should preclude any reading of Achebe as a simple case of the return of the native voice. As he says in the Conrad article, he writes from a "privileged position in African and Western cultures."[14] Consequently, *Arrow of God,* like *Heart of Darkness*, can be taken as an important instance of what Gayatri Spivak calls "the constant recoding of the culture of the West" (18) at the same time as it is contributing to the building of an African literary tradition, in the conditions that obtain at the postcolonial end of the twentieth century.

In conclusion, these debates clearly have no simple resolution in the short term; the issue between Achebe and Conrad, a politics of confrontation as opposed to a politics of subversion, the tension between textual construction and authentic being, all such debates must be kept firmly on the agenda. And so with the thorny question of racism, for all its inherent problems and because of suspicion: What are the constraints of the present that appear to condemn us to go on putting such issues in terms of mutually exclusive binary oppositions? Is there a cultural politics possible which does not require the total suppression of one set of terms in a two-sided argument?

NOTES

1. In a lecture at the University of Massachusetts, Amherst, February 18, 1975. Later published in *The Massachusetts Review*, 18, 1975, and reprinted in an amended version in Robert Kimbrough, ed., *Heart of Darkness* (New York and London: Norton, third edition, 1988). One such amendment was to alter the original phrase 'bloody racist' to 'thoroughgoing racist.'
2. Some moments of this debate include: Homi Bhabha, "Of Mimicry and Men: The Ambivalence of Colonial Discourse," October 28, 1984; Benita Parry, "Problems in Current Theories of Colonial Discourse," *Oxford Literary Review*, 9, Nos. 1-2, 1987; Gayatri Spivak, "Naming Gayatri Spivak," interview with Maria Koundoura, *Stanford Humanities Review*, 1, 1, 1989.

3. "Hybrid" is here used in the specialized sense developed by Bhabha.
4. Gayatri Spivak, "Can the Subaltern Speak?" In Gary Nelson and Lawrence Grossberg, ed., *Marxism and the Interpretation of Culture* (Urbana: University of Illinois Press, 1988).
5. Spivak, "Naming Gayatri Spivak," pp. 91-93.
6. Two important collections of essays devoted entirely to the question of racism and representation are: Henry Louis Gates, Jr., ed., *'Race', Writing and Difference* (Chicago and London: University of Chicago Press, 1986), and David Theo Goldberg, ed., *Anatomy of Racism* (Minneapolis: University of Minnesota Press, 1990).
7. This comes close to the terms of an older, Marxist critique of Conrad's politics. See, for example, Terry Eagleton, *Criticism and Ideology* (London: New Left Books, 1976), pp. 134-35.
8. In the essay, "Geography and Some Explorers," Joseph Conrad, *Tales of Hearsay and Last Essays* (London: Dent, 1955), p. 17.
9. Frederick R. Karl and Laurence Davies, ed., *The Collected Letters of Joseph Conrad* (Cambridge: Cambridge University Press, 1983), Vol. I (1861-1897), p. 319.
10. See Kimbrough, pp. 193-95.
11. *Ibid.*, p. 38.
12. *Ibid.*, p. 47.
13. Chinua Achebe, *Arrow of God* (London: Heinemann, 1964), pp. 29-30.
14. Kimbrough, p. 261.

Conrad's *Heart of Darkness* vis-a-vis Achebe's *Things Fall Apart*

AYESHA IRFAN

Heart of Darkness by Conrad is regarded as one of the greatest short novels in English language. It is said to be a significant work of modern literature. It establishes the dominant theme of twentieth century writings, that is, the fear and disillusionment about western man's place in the world and values by which he lives. Marlow, the narrator and the central character, makes a trip from "civilized" Europe to the primitive interior of the dark continent of Congo and back again. Here he encounters the demonic character of Kurtz, who is said to have been claimed by the powers of darkness. He also witnesses the violent frenzy of primitive people in the dark continent of Africa. At the same time, he comes to know about the hypocrisy of the colonizers who were exploiting the continent and its people for their own selfish purposes.

Heart of Darkness has been appreciated for giving us a true picture of the conditions in which the savages of Congo, a country of dark continent of Africa, lived under the imperialist rule of the Europeans. It is also said to give a truthful account of the behaviour and attitudes of white men, who went to that country as traders or agents of a trading company, or as explorers. If we analyze the novel closely, we find this to be a typically Eurocentric point of view of the continent, prevalent in the nineteenth century. Conrad like any other European writer was only justifying imperialist interests in the continent. By reducing the inhabitants to the level of superior monkeys, one could always justify their treatment as "beasts of burden," and thereby justify European imperialist interests on grounds of their moral duty to reform these savages.

This stereotypical image of the Africans created by novelists like Conrad is difficult to wipe out because it has a long history. As Achebe puts it, "white racism against Africa is such a normal way of thinking, that its manifestations go completely unmarked."[1] By studying the two novels *Heart of Darkness* and *Things Fall Apart* together, one can see how a colonial discourse is set into motion, and how a counter discourse is developed by emerging postcolonial writers. *Things Fall Apart* clearly shows how an inadequate account of African people and their cultures has been popularised by novels like *Heart of Darkness*. *Things Fall Apart* is one of the novels that show how psychological domination of Europeans could be resisted, or what Ngugi would call "the decolonizing of mind."

Conrad enjoys the reputation of being a liberal minded humanist for his sympathetic portrayal of the Africans. This novel has been appreciated by most of the European critics. It has been interpreted variously. The journey into the jungle symbolizes the darkness in the heart of man or potential evil in man. Jerome Thale sees the story as "the Grail quest."[2] What Marlow receives after his quest is a terrible illumination. In Kurtz Marlow discovers not simply one man become evil but a universal possibility. Kurtz lacked self restraint. Therefore, instead of reforming the savages, he became one like them. Here, the dark continent itself indirectly becomes the symbol of evil. And the lowest one can fall is to become like the inferior creatures of the continent. There are strong hints in the story that Kurtz is a good man who has gone wrong in a jungle. Kurtz has been compared to one of the greatest epic heroes, Aeneas. Like Aeneas Kurtz starts out as an emissary of light but unlike Aeneas he cannot conquer himself.

Reading *Heart of Darkness* closely, we find that the above critics give us only a limited and an essentially European viewpoint. The changing scenario in recent times has brought new perceptions and insights into African situation. Therefore, one does question the philosophical assumptions and moral values which underwrite and dictate Europe's humanist tradition. According to Achebe, *Heart of Darkness*, however well written, cannot be considered great literature because it consigned Africans to the category of subhuman and failed to recognize their full humanity. If one examines the passage given below closely, one would agree with Achebe.

> We were wanderers of prehistoric earth that wore the aspects of an unknown planet. . . . The earth seemed unearthly. We were accustomed to the shackled form of a conquered monster, but there you could look at a thing monstrous and free. It was unearthly, and the men were—No they were not inhuman. It would come slowly to one. They howled and leaped, and spun, and made horrid faces.

> But what thrilled you was just the thought of their humanity—like yours—the thought of your kinship with this wild and passionate uproar. Ugly. Yes it was ugly enough.[3]

Conrad asserts the fact that Africans are from an inferior race. Here he portrays the image of Africa "as the other world, the antithesis of Europe, where a man's vaunted intelligence and refinement are finally mocked down by triumphant bestiality."[4]

Things Fall Apart tells the story from the point of view of Africans. The people in this novel live a normal, unfrenzied life. Achebe shows how a dignified and highly developed civilization had existed before imperial domination set in. The social harmony in the village is evoked vividly, through Achebe's presentation of its customs and traditions. It shows a well-ordered and self-contained world of African society. The first part of the novel can be said to be a pastoral recollection of life. The latter part of the novel highlights the social and psychological conflicts created by the incursion of the white man and his culture into the hitherto self-contained world of African society.

In *Heart of Darkness*, Marlow gets the credit for being liberal minded because of his sympathies with the so-called "brutes." He is also critical of the hypocritical and commercial minded Englishmen on the continent, whose main purpose is to exploit the natives for the purpose of obtaining ivory. While sympathizing with the natives, Marlow points out:

> They were all dying slowly—it was clear. They were not enemies, they were not criminals, they were nothing earthly now, nothing but black shadows of disease and starvation, lying confusedly in greenish gloom. Brought from all recesses of the coast in all the legality of time contracts, lost in uncongenial surroundings, fed on unfamiliar food. They sickened, became inefficient and were then allowed to crawl away and rest. (56)

Marlow here seems to be anxious about the state of the natives but no positive alternative is offered to bring them out of their abject state. These kind of advanced humane views have helped only in the advancement of colonialism. Conrad could sympathize with these crawling creatures only because they were in their place. As Achebe points out: "for Conrad things being in their place is of utmost importance." (7) When Conrad observes another native who he feels has left his place, he can only mock at him:

> He was an improved specimen . . . to look at him was as edifying as seeing a dog in a parody of breeches and a feather hat walking on his hind legs. . . . He ought to have been clapping his hand or stamping his feet on the bank, instead of which he was hard at work, a thrall to strange witchcraft, full of improving knowledge. (58)

Reading the above passages, Marlow's sympathies with these natives sound only hypocritical. He can hardly do anything for these people when he so consciously distances himself from them. He also sees their minds as belonging to the earliest beginnings of time. They are not given the status of proper human beings who can think of their own welfare. He in fact denies them faculty of human speech. In place of speech they made only "a violent babble of uncouth sounds." They are portrayed only as dumb brutes.

The description of the two women in the novel is quite significant. One is the nameless African woman and the other is Kurtz's intended. The author has bestowed human expression to the English woman while he has withheld it from the African woman. "The woman is thought of, as an embodiment of inferior qualities of womanhood. She is emblematic representation of the continent itself in all its frenzied passion, uncontrollable, powerless, inaudible and certainly functionally inarticulate."[5] She is said to be "savage superb wild eyed . . . with an air of brooding over inscrutable purpose." (89) The European counterpart on the other hand is shown to have a mature capacity for fidelity, belief and suffering.

The African woman is deliberately denied an access to language. This only creates an unbridgeable gulf between the natives and the Europeans. Marlow passes judgements on these people without making an effort to understand them fully. It is in fact language that attracts Marlow to the demonic character of Kurtz who can speak English. Kurtz shows western man's love for power and money. Marlow shows self-restraint which Kurtz lacked. But we see that he maintains the same superiority over the natives. He assumes them to be inferior creatures without understanding them deeply.

Kurtz has lived close to the natives. So he is probably aware of the injustice done to the natives by the Europeans. In one such moment of illumination, he painted a picture of a blindfolded woman, posed against a dark background, carrying a torch that casts sinister light on her face.

This image shows Kurtz's awareness of the wrong done by him and rest of the Europeans who had shut their eyes and were busy exploiting the natives for their own purposes, though they had come to the continent to light the torch of knowledge.

Achebe, on the other hand, proves in his novel that Africans are not primitive people and that African history is not "one long night of savagery." (30) He emphasizes the fact that colonial domination of a more technologically advanced society cannot be excused on ethical grounds of reforming a less advanced society. Achebe writes: African people did not hear of culture for the first time from Europeans, that their societies were not mindless, but frequently had a philosophy of great depth and beauty, that they had poetry and above all they had dignity. It is this dignity many African people lost in the colonial period."[6]

Achebe does not fail to analyze the weaknesses of their society, of which the Europeans had taken advantage in order to exploit them. In this society, fear of gods and evil often motivate the Africans towards many acts of brutality. Twins are taken by the Ibos as the very embodiment of evil. They are abandoned alive in the evil forest. The commands of gods are carried out without any question. In fact the disintegration of character of Okonkwo begins when he murders the child who looks at him as his own father. Okonkwo's own son Nwoye is repulsed by this action of his father. He forsakes his father and his values and joins the new faith of Christianity which stands for universal brotherhood and self-knowledge. The other members of the society, like the parents of the twins or those who are held in contempt by the society, take refuge in the new faith brought to the village by the missionaries.

Things Fall Apart further emphasizes the fact that African society would have changed for the better without European interference. The Ibo society was not inert. Change here was subtle, like the change in the punishment for breaking the peace of Ani. Okonkwo who beats his wife during the peace week is ordered by the priest of earth goddess Ani to bring to her shrine only some fine. Ezeudu, one of the oldest men of the village, tells two men who come to visit him that the punishment for breaking peace of Ani has become quite mild. It had not always been so: "he had been told that in the past a man who broke the peace was dragged on this ground until he died. But after a while this custom was stopped because it spoilt the peace which it was meant to preserve."[7]

The people of Umurao in *Arrow of God* can cite numerous examples of customs that had been changed in the past, when they began to work hardships on the lives of people. Left to itself, the Ibo society would have changed slowly and naturally. But the change that was triggered off by the advent of white man in the village was too sudden for Ibo clan to cope with. Therefore, it led to the rapid disintegration of its culture. The tragic climax of the book is the result of a direct conflict between the mythical gods and the Christian god. The iconoclastic religion, which Okonkwo calls "lunatic religion," shatters all their beliefs, superstitions and customs.

The breaking up of traditional culture in the face of the new religion is confirmed by happenings such as the construction of church in the "Evil forest," the bringing up of twins, cutting up of long hair, etc. by the missionaries without any harmful effects on them. Traditionally such things were not done for the fear of death. The people in the village see things as "breaking up and falling apart." (167) Oberika laments, "Now he has won our brothers and the clan can no longer act like one. He has put a knife on things that held us together and we have fallen apart." (160)

The killing of the sacred royal python by a convert and the unmasking of one of the "egwugwu" again by a convert, call for a direct confrontation between the natives and the whites, who have now established their own government and judicial system in the village. The harassment of the leader of Umuofia by the officials of the government further leads to acts of reprisal in which Okonkwo severs the head of one messenger. His action is not approved by his fellow clansmen. His fight, he feels, is a war of blame. The best way he finds of facing it is by hanging himself.

The Englishmen slowly gain the political control of the natives. The book ends with the district commissioner planning the title of the book that he is writing as "The Pacification of Primitive Tribes in Lower Niger." This British officer can be seen plainly as no more than a typically short-sighted, late victorian colonial officer who is justifying the British imperialist interests and the exploitation of the natives in ethical terms. This kind of thinking dominated the minds of the major European countries and is reflected in *Heart of Darkness*.

NOTES

1. Chinua Achebe, *Hopes and Impediments* (New York: Anchor, 1988), p. 12.

2. Jerome Thale, "Marlow's Quest," *Heart of Darkness: An Authoritative Text Background and Sources of Criticism*, ed. R. Kimbrough (New York: Morton, 1971), p. 176.
3. Joseph Conard, *Heart of Darkness* (New Delhi: UBS, 1994).
4. *Hopes and Impediments*, p. 3.
5. Y. Asante, "(Re)Discovering Europe," *In Between: Essays and Studies in Literary Criticism*, vol. 2, March 1993, p. 20.
6. Chinua Achebe, "The Role of the Writers in New Nation," *Nigerian Magazine*, 1964, p. 157.
7. Chinua Achebe, *Things Fall Apart* (New Delhi: Arnold Heinemann, 1987), p. 29.

Culture and Anarchy in Chinua Achebe's *Things Fall Apart*

V. JAYALAKSHMI

In his novel *Things Fall Apart*, the well-known Nigerian writer Chinua Achebe draws one's attention to the cultural glory and the subsequent downfall of an African native society. In moving fictional terms, he exposes the anarchic tendencies that led to the degeneration of an erstwhile rich culture. According to Sri Aurobindo, any culture that gives up "its living separateness and neglects an active self-defence will be swallowed up and the nation which lived by it will lose its soul and perish."[1]

History tells us that great civilizations such as the Chinese, Egyptian and Roman, flourished and yet failed to survive the test of time evidently because of the lack of 'living separateness.' A culture can retain its identity only if it is flexible enough to take in changes and assimilate from other cultures. On the other hand, if it becomes inert and rigid, then, the scourge of disorder sweeps it off leaving behind 'mere anarchy.'

In all societies, there are certain basic values which need to be perpetuated. These values give a culture its identity. So, loss of culture means loss of identity for a society. Perfection is possible only by growing and becoming in the light of reason and wisdom. Only then a society can develop a lasting culture, safe-guarding it from the threat of anarchy either by external interference or by internal tensions. This, in brief, is an important theme that dominates Achebe's first but most remarkable novel, *Things Fall Apart*. It is structured on a limited frame of 148 pages. Yet, it tells of the hitherto unknown phases of African life. The novel is located at the turn of the nineteenth century. The whites have just entered the dark continent and are exploring the possibilities of expanding their power.

Things Fall Apart is the story of an Ibo warrior and his society, told in three parts. It reveals in its course the friction within the individual and the society, and the way both account for the transformation that their culture undergoes. Its values have been put to test due to "stresses generated from outside through friction with new sets of values and institutional structures."[2]

Okonkwo, the protagonist, typifies the Ibo society to a large extent. He is a fine product of a society, the culture of which demands unquestioning loyalty to the clan's ethic in its daily existence. Okonkwo starts supporting himself and his family from a tender age, thus laying foundations for a prosperous future. His society considers achievement more important than age. Accordingly, Okonkwo, as a young man of eighteen brought honour to himself and to his village by defeating a famous wrestler. He also proved his calibre by fighting in several wars. His resilience of mind is also put to test during the time of drought. While some farmers hanged themselves out of desperation, Okonkwo, with great forethought, goes to a rich farmer to borrow some yam seedlings. Nwakibie, a prudent elder, knows about Okonkwo's ability and lends him some yams without hesitation. As the Ibos say, Okonkwo broke his palm kernels himself and his 'chi' agreed. Thus, Okonkwo exemplifies the male values of his society such as fearlessness and inflexible will. Like the great Ghengz Khan, he rises from rags to riches by sheer willpower and stamina.

But the fact remains that Okonkwo's relentless effort in search of riches and respect is motivated by his fear of being compared to his no-good idler father, Unoka. As a result Okonkwo 'threw' himself into the task of building a 'prosperous future,' 'like one possessed.' Fear of failure makes him hate the qualities of his father i.e. gentleness and kindness. In the process, he denies compassion and forgiveness as well.

Besides suffering from fear complex, Okonkwo lacks a comprehensive understanding of his clan's ethic which places equal importance on male and female values. As Abiola Irele says, "It is the need to live down the shame of his father that compels him to an excessive adherence to the social code to an extent which in fact transforms a value into a weakness."[3]

The element of anarchy in Okonkwo is particularly evident when the Oracles of Hills and Caves order the death of Ikemefuna. Despite the village elder, Ezeudu's warning, Okonkwo joins in killing the boy hostage, just to prove his manliness. When Ikemefuna runs to him for help, Okonkwo, for fear of his softer emotions taking control, quickly cuts him down. At this moment of clash between his male and female values, his fear of being thought weak, wins. He fails to find balance between individual and tribal values and he doesn't realize that rules and values need not be mutually exclusive.

Violence and irrational nature contribute to Okonkwo's anarchy. This is proved during the week of peace. Much against the rule, Okonkwo loses his temper and beats his wife for a small mistake. It happens again when Ekwefi, his favourite wife, mocks at his dubious skill at shooting. He shoots at her in a fit of anger. For Okonkwo, the only emotion worth showing is anger. It is the same inability to resist the urge to be aggressive, especially in public, causes him grief. His gun goes berserk during the funeral rites of Ezeudu, a village elder, killing his son. Suggesting that Okonkwo's misdeed is more than an accident, Palmer argues: "It exemplifies his predisposition to violence which at last finds an outlet, and is the climax to a cumulative process."[4]

Okonkwo never tries to be rational. His lack of thinking makes his views rather superficial. For example, while discussing the strangeness in the deaths of Ndule and his wife Ozemena, Obierica recalls that Ndule could not do anything without telling his wife.

> 'I did not know that,' said Okonkwo. 'I thought he was a strong man in his youth.'
> 'He was indeed,' said Ofoedu.
> Okonkwo shook his head doubtfully.
> 'He led Umuofia to war in those days,' said Obierika.[5]

The single track of Okonkwo's mind could not go beyond its narrow confines to those civilized outlying areas where husband treats wife as his equal, friend and guide. He fails to see the union of Ndule and Ozeomena as symbolic of the harmony of the masculine and feminine principles: "it is this union men as Ndule and Ezeudu are able to achieve and which Umuofia respects and seeks in its leaders."[6]

Okonkwo lacks warmth and enthusiasm in personal relations. During the New Yam feast, he has nothing much to say to his kinsmen while Obierika greets at least half a dozen men. Even on a happy occasion, Okonkwo deliberately tries to keep himself aloof. This shows his psychological distance from others. His way of trying to become a man of success rather than a man of value further adds to his anarchy.

During his days of exile, despite the fact that he made an admirable effort to pull himself together and spring back to a prosperous life, his rashness in misjudging his people and his failure to view the missionaries rationally are indiscreet. He is unfairly rude to his son Nwoye. William Walsh rightly observes: "Okonkwo's error, the Aristotelian flaw, for this is the kind of hero he is, is to suppose that the present is wholly susceptible to his governing, moulding will."[7] Okonkwo fails to realize that a man of equanimity alone can control the events moulding them to his nature.

But there is another side to Okonkwo, which is as curious as the one that is obvious. His gentle qualities surface intermittently in spite of his effort to choke them. For instance, when Ekwefi, being unable to live with her first husband, leaves him and goes to Okonkwo, he doesn't disappoint her. Similarly, when his daughter falls ill, he dares going into the bush in the middle of the night to fetch medicinal leaves for her. Again when Ikemefuna is put to death, Okonkwo is torn with remorse for two days. Okonkwo's effort and aim to become prosperous without letting his personal worries affect him is indeed admirable. Even in exile, he becomes a successful farmer, marries two more wives and gets more children. He likes the grand old ways of kinship and generosity. He invites his kinsmen of Mbanta to a moonlit dinner to offer them his 'little kola' i.e. his gratitude for their kindness. He, being a man of forethought, plans his return well in advance.

Okonkwo finds the changes in Umuofia due to the advent of the white man meaningless. He feels the strangers could have been driven away easily with clansmen's war-like attitude. He now becomes concerned about the changes that are taking place among his people. He forgets his personal matters such as stabilizing his rank and status and introducing his sons into the Ozo title-taking society. As a man of absolute loyalty to his culture, Okonkwo "mourned for the warlike men of Umuofia, who had so unaccountably become soft like women." (129) However, Okonkwo retrieves his war-like mein and respect of his clansmen when he along with other 'egwugwu' destroys the church, in order to atone for the crime committed by an over-zealous convert i.e. unmasking an ancestral spirit.

Okonkwo's pride suffers a great shock when he, along with four others, is arrested and humiliated for three days. His last act of tragedy is mainly on account of the white DC's dastardly action of insulting and injuring the pride of the warriors of Umuofia. "As he lay on his bamboo bed he thought about the treatment he received in the white man's court, and he swore vengeance. If Umuofia decided on war, all would be well. But they chose to be cowards he would go out and avenge himself." (141)

The values of Ibo culture are best realized in Okonkwo who now lives for the sole purpose of his clan's survival. On the next day, when the clansmen assemble for deliberations, a court messenger of the white man interrupts it. Unable to bear with it and with a spirit of war descending on him, Okonkwo kills him. Clansmen fall back in fear. Tragically, here Okonkwo's hopes for his clan's survival meet with the dismal attitude of his people. He is made to realize that valour and courage of the clan are now things of past. Instead of breaking into war, they retreat in fear. It is ironic that fear, which is Okonkwo's flaw has now taken over the entire clan. Achebe comments: "the conflict between Okonkwo and the clan arises because Okonkwo remains true to the ideals which gave him heroic stature while the clan changes its loyalties."[8]

Okonkwo decides to remove himself from the scene rather than living like a slave under alien rule. Majestically dressed in his war gear, Okonkwo is found behind his compound hanging from a tree even as Shakespeare's Cleopatra is found dead in queenly splendour. His "final protest at fate leaves a lasting impression on his people and therein lies his eventual triumph."[9]

Despite his heroic act which affirms his faith in his culture, it is Okonkwo's basic lack of reasoning that brings him to his tragic end. He never pauses to think about the 'unaccountable' effiminacy of the clansmen. Also, he doesn't change with age and experience: "as a man he is dedicated to the same stereotypes he formed in his youth."[10] The clan's ethic recognized only those who never bent. Accordingly Okonkwo thwarted his finer emotions such as love, compassion and a humanitarian point of view. This has obliterated his growth as a complete man, leaving him without a sense of fulfilment and freedom. This in turn has made him vulnerable to the onslaught of anarchy.

It is the height of tragic irony that Okonkwo's body is shunned by his clansmen, because his death by suicide is considered an abomination according to their culture. Thus the tragedy of Okonkwo symbolizes both the facets of society, its culture and its anarchy at the individual and the communal levels.

The traditional culture of Umuofia is rich enough in its religion, philosophy, poetry and art. Achebe affirms: "African people did not hear of culture for the first time from Europeans; that their societies were not mindless but frequently had a philosophy of great depth and value and beauty, that they had poetry and above all they had dignity."[11]

The religious tradition of the Ibo culture falls neatly into three clearly defined areas. First, worship and rituals of traditional deities, including the Oracles of the Hills and Caves, secondly the worship of ancestors and finally the concept of 'chi' that occupies a place of great importance in the Ibo cosmology.

The Ibo attitude advocates participation in practical life and stresses at the same time an awareness of the dead, the living and the future generation: "The religious sense thus not only maintains social equilibrium but also creates a sense of continuity. African traditional life is not thus divided rigidly into the sacred and the secular. Religion gives direction and completion to their scheme of life."[12]

The Ibo system of worship is elaborately designed. Chukwu, the supreme god, broods over creation rather than participating in it. Ani or Ala is the earth goddess. She is more influential than all other deities. She embodies all female values such as kindness and charity. She is the custodian of all arts. The earth goddess is honoured at all important ceremonies such as the New Yam Feast. People thank her for giving them her plenty, by offering the new yam. All possible offences are checked and the menace of anarchy is kept at bay by adherence to the prescribed rites and rituals of Ani. Thus, for an inadvertent sin such as killing a kinsman, banishment is the punishment. Okonkwo is exiled for seven years when he accidentally kills a young man. He has to flee the village for desecrating the earth-goddess. For deliberate sins such as suicide which is a greater abomination, the retributory measure is even more severe. Such a man's body is untouchable for the clansmen; therefore, his last rites are performed by strangers as in the case of Okonkwo.

The Oracles of Hills and Caves is represented by a deity called Agbala. Clansmen seek solutions for their problems from the possessed priestess of the deity. It warns them of the coming of the white man. Its prophetic power thus keeps the people vigilant.

The second salient feature of the Ibo religion is ancestor worship. The spirits of the ancestors, whose bodies are committed to earth are associated with the Earth Goddess, and therefore with every ceremony held in her honour, or with the funeral function of an important elder, as that of Ezeudu, they emerge to participate. Eminent members of the community impersonate as the ancestors. These are the 'egwugwu' who represent the nine villages of Umuofia. They appear in awe-inspiring costumes, speaking an esoteric tongue. They also hold land's highest court. It ensures the unity and peace of the clan.

The third important feature of Ibo religion is the concept of 'chi.' The 'chi' is believed to be the guardian spirit granted to every individual at the time of his birth. It is believed to be a part of the individual's 'supreme creative essence' and therefore responsible for the good and bad of one's life. Thus Okonkwo's 'chi' helps him in making his life a success. But when he exceeds limits, his 'chi' takes over and his 'inflexible will' brings him to a sad end. The concept of 'chi' thus conveys a highly developed code of ethics as the apotheosis of the age-old wisdom of the Ibo culture. Thus the triad as a whole and the male, female values rule the material, moral and the spiritual planes of the Ibo world.

Although there is no centre of authority, the nine villages of Umuofia are unified through marriage, title taking ceremonies, feasts and adherence to the proclamations. They are also bound by the same code of justice, political matters, ceremonies marking birth, marriage and death, tribal conflicts, markets and meetings.

The Ibo culture believes in the saying 'mother is supreme.' In times of crisis, a man seeks solace at his mother's place. Thus, when Okonkwo flees his home overnight, he goes to Mbanta, his mother's village. Similarly when a man dies, his body is taken to his mother's people for last rites. Traditionally women are neither inferior nor superior to men. They are economically independent. They grow their own crops and hold their own markets.

According to Ibo culture, communal ethic is considered greater than that of the individual, as in the case of Ikemefuna, the boy hostage from Mbaino. On the other hand, people join hands to help a man out of crisis as in the case of Okonkwo and others. The villagers unite and raise funds to get them released from the white man's prison.

Ibo purpose of art is twiborn. For them art is not only aesthetically fulfilling but it is also functional. Music and dance are an integral part of an Ibo man's life. For every occasion there is a song and a dance to go with. There is a wide variety of songs ranging from songs of wedding, of harvest, of funeral to songs of rain. During the windy harmattan, children sing,

> the rain is falling
> the rain is falling
> Alone Nnade is cooking and eating. (25)

Nwoye romanticizes that Nnade perhaps belongs to that colourful world in which the ant holds his court in splendour and the 'sands dance forever.' The fragrance of Ibo poetry of Umuofia is highly appealing. After the white advent, the people of Umuofia make songs of mockery directed against the court messengers. The flute and the drum provide the background for nearly all occasions. The variety of drums such as the Ekwe, Udu and Ogene are used not only for entertainment but also to deliver messages and announce important proclamations. It is an inseparable part of a man's life. It is used to celebrate birth, marriage, wrestling contests, title taking ceremonies and feasts. It reflects the pulse of the clan's life. In Umuofia there is a saying, "As the man danced, so the drums were beaten for him." (121) It signifies the truth that will and destiny of a man are interlinked. A wrestling match with its drum beat "was like the pulsation of its heart. It throbbed in the air, in the sunshine, and even in the trees, and filled the village with excitement." (321) The language of the drum is a fascinating feature of the Ibo aesthetics. No wonder the most sophisticated version of this instrument and its operation have their origin in the remote jungles of Africa.

Like the Olympic games which were an expression of the love of sports and adventure in the ancient Greeks, the harvesting time provides the atmosphere for the spirit of sport which represents agility and courage of the Ibos. The art of oratory is regarded a special talent. A good speaker is he who is blessed with a deep and steady voice that reaches a large crowd. His language must carry a good number of proverbs as 'the palm oil with which words are eaten.' In Umuofia there are a number of such speakers.

It is noteworthy that the well-knit ethic of Umuofia guarantees economic security, political safety and religious sanctity to all. With the taking over of power crazy 'people of the world' anarchy enters its fold:

> Turning and turning in the widening gyre
> The falcon cannot see the falconer;
> Things fall apart; the centre cannot hold;
> Mere anarchy is loosed upon the world.[13]

Achebe could not have chosen a better title for his novel meant to awaken his people. In his attempt to show the good that passed away from his culture, he doesn't gloss over the unsavoury details. He admits "like other people's pasts ours had its good as well as its bad sides."[14]

One of the main issues that caused 'things' to fall in the native society is the disharmony in the sphere of religion. For example, the Oracles of Hills and Caves which often deliver harsh justice, clash directly with female values such as charity and compassion represented by Ani, the earth goddess. The parctice of harsh justice still continues. If a cow strays into someone's compound its owner is forced to pay fine while the real culprits are some children. The same injustice is seen when Okonkwo is exiled for an inadvertent sin but escapes punishment when he deliberately shoots at his wife.

Primitive customs such as the throwing away of twins as they are regarded an abomination, abandoning victims of swelling disease to die a lonely death and mutilation of 'ogbange' children reveal a strong streak of anarchy. Here is a culture that carries on human sacrifices and encourages bloodshed and violence in the name of valour and manliness, a society that regards a child valuable, condemns him to death to keep its rigid laws and customs. It is this dichotomy that finally leads Okonkwo to wrong perceptions of his culture causing overwhelming anarchy. As Solomon Iyasere points out, "Outwardly, Umuofia is a world of serenity, harmony and communal activities but inwardly it is torn by individual's personal doubts and fears." (75)

When the whites start living in the 'evil forest' without mishap, for first time doubts spark off among the natives about their religion. The white man not only disproves their established myths but also provides answers to their questions relating to the outcastes called Osus and the issue of throwing away of twins. The new religion, Christianity, harbours not only sensitive and unsuccessful people like Nwoye but also mothers of twins and Osus. The Ibo religion lacks tolerance and instead of raising the weak, it abandons them to their miserable fate.

The coming of the white man also marks the end of a heroic era. Fear of the white man's power robs the natives of courage and manliness. Obierika sums up the situation thus: "the white man came quietly and peaceably with his religion. We were amused at his foolishness and allowed him to stay. Now he has won our brothers, and our clan can no longer act like one. He had put a knife on the things that held us together and we have fallen apart." (124-25) The same gravity is reiterated by an elder while thanking Okonkwo for his dinner. He says, "I fear for you, young people because you do not understand how strong is the bond of kinship. You do not know what it is to speak with one voice and what is the result? An abominal religion has settled among you." (118) These passages indicate the bitter truth that the clansmen are as much responsible as the white man in turning the odds against the Ibo society.

The ancient culture of Umuofia is most unaware of the snare of confusion set by the falconer, the white men, in addition to the existing danger of anarchy within the clan itself. The lapses within the native culture help the strangers to lay inroads into it. The white man does his best to baffle the natives who have no idea of the outside world. As Bruce Macdonald observes, "For the people of Umuofia, caught between the degeneration of their own system of social and religious orientation and the imperfectly understood process of the new order, the world is indeed anarchy, and it is this anarchy which Okonkwo attempts to overcome with his last heroic act." (56)

With the disappearance of a proud clan, a new set of 'efelefu' or worthless men sprout all over Umuofia dancing to the tune called by the pale faced strangers. The integrity and innocence of the natives give way to greed for money and a craving for paid jobs. Kinship disappears with the disintegration of the family ties. Spiritual values are eroded by material comforts which in turn lead to the break up of the society. People like Okonkwo find their own ways of salvaging their self-respect. For the white D.C. who fails to see the glory of the Umuofian society, it is one of the 'primitive tribes of the Lower Niger.' He, however, concedes to allot a paragraph to the incident of Okonkwo for the reader's interest. He is unaware that the significance of that paragraph is not limited to Okonkwo alone but it symbolizes the fate of many colonized people and their vanquished heroes.

With commendable restraint, Achebe proves that things fall apart because of failure of two systems to understand each other. Instead of proving their worth, they allow anarchy to corrupt their civilized modes of perception, as evidenced by the impulsive and irrational nature in the native society and the imposing and acquisitive nature in the western society.

Things Fall Apart is Achebe's most successful attempt portraying the humanism and grandeur of the culture of the Ibo land. The novel unfolds the systematic process of destruction wrought upon the African societies by the anarchic forces in the native and alien cultures alike.

NOTES

1. Sri Aurobindo, *The Foundations of Indian Culture* (Pondicherry: Sri Aurobindo Ashram, 1980), p. 3.
2. Bu-Buakei Jabbi, "Fire and Transition in *Things Fall Apart*," *Critical Perspectives on Chinua Achebe*, p. 135.
3. Abiola Irele, "The Tragic Conflict in the Novels of Chinua Achebe,"

Critical Perspectives on Chinua Achebe, ed. C.L. Innes and B. Lindfors (London: Heinemann, 1979), p. 11.

4. Eustace Palmer, "Chinua Achebe," *An Introduction to the African Novel* (London: Heinemann, 1972), p. 55.
5. Chinua Achebe, *Things Fall Apart* (1958; rpt. London: Heinemann, 1983), p. 48.
6. Solomon O. Iyasere, "Narrative Techniques in *Things Fall Apart*," *Critical Perspectives on Chinua Achebe*, p. 104.
7. William Walsh, *A Manifold Voice* (London: Chatto and Windus, 1970), p. 50.
8. Bruce F. Macdonald, "Chinua Achebe and the Structure of Colonial Tragedy," *The Literary Half-Yearly*, XXI, 1, January 1980, p. 55.
9. Josephine Leach, "A Study of Chinua Achebe's *Things Fall Apart* in Mid-America," *English Journal*, 60 (1971), p. 1054.
10. Solomon Iyasere, "Narrative Techniques in *Things Fall Apart*."
11. Chinua Achebe, "The Role of the Writer in New Nation," *African Writers on African Writing*, ed. G.D. Killam (London: Heinemann, 1973), p. 8.
12. Emelia Aseme Oko, "The Historical Novel of Africa," *The Conch*, 6, 1-2 (1974), p. 22.
13. W.B. Yeats, "The Second Coming," *The Premier Book of Major Poems: An Anthology*, ed. Anita Dore (New York: Fawcett, 1970), p. 48.
14. Chinua Achebe, "Role of the Writer in a New Nation," p. 9.

Community Called Quest: Chinua Achebe's *No Longer at Ease*

V.T. GIRDHARI

"He who has people is richer than he who has money,"[1] says the old man who greeted his native village Umuofia in a war like salute. The old man's statement is suggestive of the pride of the community unity with which it stands by an individual during crisis; but the statement also exposes the greater truth about community's possessive attitude towards individual. In *No Longer at Ease* Achebe assesses the community's relation with its own ideals resulting in tension between community and the individual. Nigeria of Achebe is a society where traditional-cultural values still retain their power. Achebe's choice of the title from T.S. Eliot's "The Journey of the Magi" explains the protagonist's state of mind. Obiajulu Okonkwo is "no longer at ease, in the old dispensation" ("The Journey of the Magi"). The novel deals directly with distress and difficulty of the individual amidst contemporary social, economic and political problems of Africa. James Booth observes: "Obi, Achebe's representative of the new elite is caught between the remnants of colonialism and his ill-educated fellow countrymen."[2]

Obi represents a people, a value system and is the victim of the circumstances that have been responsible for his birth and growth. Umuofia's community that had financed his education in England expect him not only to repay that "scholarship" but return the favour in form of some activities for betterment of the community. They had sent him to study law so that he could handle all their land cases against their neighbours. When Joshua loses his job, the community expects from Obi to fix him up in a suitable situation since Obi now holds a European post. "We now have one of our sons in the senior services. . . . It is in little things like this that he can help us." (79) What they don't realize is, observes David Carroll, that, "the knowledge which brings power also brings detachment and alienation."[3] Carroll calls Obi "a black Englishman" whose English education has given him a greater insight into African corruptions and therefore, distanced him from his tribe.

Achebe's concerns, obviously, lean towards the community rather than the individual. For him it is a group-consciousness that counts; individual is just a part of the machine, unrepresentative of the whole. S.A. Khayyoom remarks: "The isolation of the individual in African novel makes him exceptional, whereas the loneliness of the protagonist in the western novel makes him typical and representative of his society. . . . It is the will of the majority that consciously contributes towards a coherent and organic African society. But the problem for a sensitive, self-conscious creative being is how to delink himself from his group and to assert his individuality."[4]

Obi, before leaving for England, had been warned by his tradition-bound community elders that the native young man who married a white woman was "lost to his people. He is like rain wasted in the forest." (18) So, on his return from England when he falls in love with Clara, an Osu, his parents and people take it as an audacious act of defiance. How could a son of the Umuofia who had come back to join community's march "towards political irredentism, social equality and economic emancipation" (37) could ever think of love with a woman outside their clan? There was time when Obi himself thought of love as another "grossly overrated European invention." (70) But that was before he met Clara. And now European education had made him stranger in his own community. He did not comprehend his childhood friend Joseph when he said that Clara was an Osu, an outcast, and therefore Obi could not marry her.

To the English trained mind of Obi, it all seemed "scandalous" (72) that in the middle of the twentieth century one could not marry a girl just because some of her ancestors had dedicated themselves to serve a God. The pressure of the community on the individual amounts, sometimes, to blackmail. Obi's people, for instance, are willing to grant him longer period for repayment of loan scholarship, but, "I have heard," says the President, "that you are moving around with a girl of doubtful ancestry and even thinking of marrying her." (82) Obi's father tells him point blank, "You can't marry the girl." (125) Even Obi's mother, his last straw to stick to, does not mince words. She very plainly tells him, "If you do the thing while I am alive, you will have my blood on your head, because I shall kill myself." (29) Both parents understand the nobility of Clara's parents but Ibu and Osu can never meet. James Booth analyzes it aptly when he observes: "It is his European education which makes him so contemptuously reject the taboo against marrying the Osu or outcast, Clara, while those to whom he is indebted for his education, the villagers of Umuofia, are ironically the sternest upholders of the taboo." (99) Obi gratefully acknowledges his clan's contribution that provided him with the best education at a great expense; but the best part of the education he acquired in England was indomitable independence of the individual.

Cultural orthodoxy of the elders causes so much suffocation to the youngsters that the community attitude brings Obi-Clara relationship to the catastrophic stage. Clara feels so humiliated at the familial and social rejection that she not only breaks off the engagement but does not feel it necessary to tell Obi about his child she is carrying. She prefers to suffer alone. Achebe, through the collapse of Obi-Clara relationship, suggests that the individual's failure to come to terms with community ideals is directly consequential to the utter prostration of his own ideals. Carroll calls it a conflict between "European individualism and African tribalism." (76)

The peace that finally dawns upon Obi is the peace of death. Achebe tells us that "Beyond death there are no ideals and no hum—but, only reality . . . we all have to stand on the earth itself and go with her pace." (156)

Earth, for Achebe, is a symbol for community mind which is a reality. Individual has to go on living, forced within that frame and still be at peace. Learning to live with community ideals is like accepting the idea of death. After his mother's death and Clara's walk-out, Obi recalls the story of king David who refused food when his beloved son was sick, but washed and ate when he died. David must have felt the same kind of peace, broods Obi in the end, "the peace that passeth all understanding." (154) For Achebe Obi's is "an inevitable tragedy." Booth sums it up well: "It seemed that was the way Nigeria was built." (97)

NOTES

1. Chinua Achebe, *No Longer at Ease* (New York: Fawcett, 1960), p. 79.
2. James Booth, *Writings and Politics in Nigeria* (London: Hodder and Stoughton, 1981), p. 90.
3. David Carroll, *Chinua Achebe: Novelist, Poet, Critic* (London: Macmillan, 1990), p. 65.
4. S.A. Khayyoom, "The Neo-Anthropological Novels of Chinua Achebe" in *Commonwealth Fiction*, ed. R.K. Dhawan (New Delhi: Classical, 1988), pp. 29-30.

Amaechina (Let the Path-Never-Close) Achebe's *Anthills of the Savannah*

INDRASENA REDDY

Anthills of the Savannah[1] is a critique on the power apparatus in a neo-colonial situation. The novel also serves as an antidote to the ugly march of Power. Achebe tries to accomplish this objective not through the prescription of a class-war, or Fanonist violence, but by means of incessant struggles, the forms of which are embodied in the indigenous myths and legends.

The novelist uses the myth of the Sun (symbolized in Sam) whose power of scorching heat destroys everything around. The destructive nature of the Sun creates a terrible drought in Abazon, forcing its leadership to visit H.E. for the redressal of their problem caused by the drought. The second most powerful myth is related to the Pillar of Water (Beatrice in the context of the novel) which seeks to put out the fire of the Sun and also quench the thirst of the parched lands (of Abazon). Corruption-prone and monstrous masculine power is sought to be checkmated by Idemili, God's daughter. Achebe succinctly portrays this legend of male-power which is sought to be neutralised through female resistance:

> In the beginning Power rampaged through our world, naked. So the Almighty, looking at his creation through the round undying eye of the Sun, saw and pondered and finally decided to send his daughter, Idemili, to bear witness to the moral nature of authority by wrapping around Power's rude waist a loincloth of peace and modesty. (102)

The twin-myths of the Sun and the Pillar of Water reinforce "Idemili's contempt for man's unquenchable thirst to sit in authority on his fellows." (102) The unrestrained naked dance of Power is sought to be countered by means of struggle motif in the novel. Beatrice passionately pleads with Chris once again to sort out all his problems with Ikem to save the latter from the impending danger to his life. But the sad truth is that Chris himself is in trouble and his position in the Cabinet has already become vulnerable. His dilemma is that he can neither quit his position, nor can he fight from within. He is summoned by H.E. and pressurized to serve orders of suspension on Ikem for the latter's alleged subversive activities. As Chris refuses to comply, H.E. gets the orders of suspension served on Ikem signed by some one else.

Following his suspension from the Gazette, Ikem is determined to fight openly the fascist regime to the last. In this process, he also manages to de-alienate himself paving the way for his reassimilation into the mainstream of his nation's life and its history. He joins the delegation from Abazon at the Presidential Palace. It comprised no more than half a dozen elders of Abazon. But they were also joined by a fairly large crowd of Abazonians living in Bassa (the capital of Kangan). This delegation and the 'motley-crowd' of people send shock-waves to H.E. The unlettered and anonymous leader of the delegation addresses the crowd. His talk is subtly couched in riddles, myths, legends and parables—the very essence of age-old wisdom as embodied in the oral-lore of the land. He begins his talk by saying: "It is proper that a beggar should visit a king. . . . It is the place of the poor man to visit the rich man who holds the yam and the knife." (127) That the very people who legitimize the authority of those in power should be disgraced as beggars is a sad commentary on the nexus between the people and the rulers. The old man also ridicules the idea of Sam wanting to become the President-for-Life. He affirms that there can be no permanent arrangement in the scheme of things. Even a marriage, he opines, becomes null-and-void the moment one of the partners dies.

It seems as if the sixth sense of the old man tells him that H.E. is not likely to respond positively to their sufferings and grievances. He obliquely drops hints exhorting the Abazonians to prepare themselves for yet another "show-down" if it becomes inevitable. His message emphasizing on the 'battle,' 'the battle-cry' and the 'story' which alone survives both 'war and warrior' is very striking and significant. He says:

> The sounding of the battle-drum is important; the fierce waging of the war itself is important; and the telling of the story afterwards—each is important in its own way. I tell you there is not one of them we could do without. But if you ask me which of them

> takes the eagle-feather I will say boldly: the story . . . only the story can continue beyond the war and the warrior. It is the story that outlives the sound of war-drums and the exploits of brave fighters. It is the story, not the others, that saves our progeny from blundering like blind beggars into the spikes of the cactus fence. The story is our escort; without it we are blind. Does the blind man own his escort? No, neither do we the story; rather it is the story that owns us and directs us. (123-24)

The unlettered man's stress on the "story" as the 'escort,' and as a lesson to be learnt from the past experiences is very revealing. 'The story,' in other words, is the history of a people's past, their glorious moments and sufferings, and the record (oral or written) of their heroic resistance to all forms of oppression and exploitation.

The Abazonian elder concludes his talk with a fantastic parable related to the age-old animosity between the leopard and the tortoise. The parable is as follows: the leopard is always on the look out for the tortoise wanting to kill him. When the latter is about to be killed, he pleads with his killer to leave him alone for a minute or two enabling him to prepare himself mentally for his death. The death-wish of the tortoise is generously conceded. Meanwhile, the tortoise begins to kick, rove and throw dust in different directions. The leopard is intrigued at the crazy behaviour of the tortoise and asks the latter if he has something up his sleeve. The tiny animal says: "Because even after I am dead I would want anyone passing by this spot to say, yes, a fellow and his match struggled here." (128) The story-teller is also conscious of the fact that the struggle in the offing between the ruthless state-power and the unarmed beggars like them is uneven and is doomed to be a failure. And yet, the old man insists that the spirit of the struggle has to be kept alive as a living lesson to posterity. He observes as he wounds up his talk: "My people, that is all we are doing now. Struggling to no purpose except that those who come after us will be able to say: True, our fathers were defeated but they tried." (128) The old man receives a standing ovation from the assembly of the Abazonians. The old man's talk tremendously influences the thought-processes of the highly-educated Ikem. Folktales, songs, their inventors-cum-performers are considered to be a challenge to state power and its minions. Folk-lore and its performing artists are essentially subversive in terms of their message and mode of conduct.

The kind of response to the old-man's talk and Ikem's presence there are viewed seriously by Sam and his sycophants. Matters precipitate and come to a head-on-collision between state-power and those who are ranged against it. The story-teller and his associates are arrested and thrown behind the bars at the Bassa Maximum Security Prison. Ikem is invited to a function organized by the Bassa University Students' Union on the campus. He titled his lecture: "The Tortoise and the Leopard—a Political Meditation on the Imperative of Struggle" (153).

He began his lecture on a note of sarcasm and said: "story tellers are a threat. They threaten all champions of control, they frighten usurpers of the right-to-freedom of the human spirit—in state, in church or mosque, in party congress, in the university or wherever." (153) The message contained in this passage comes home to us all the more with a much greater relevance as we are a witness to, if not participants in, the sordid drama of struggle between state-power and the organisations ranged against it, albeit their limitations and weaknesses.

Ikem's lecture covers a wide range of topics, events, matters, personalities and state-power. He is critical of the breed of parasites—the university students and the faculty. He indicts the faculty for priding on its parasitism and for their incorrigible habit of parroting the text-book oriented theories on revolution, Marxism and the like ignoring the functional aspect of it. He seems to be of the view that knowledge of a theory however great and magnificent, suffers seriously in the hands of its pseudo-ideologues (with whom our universities are littered).

Ikem assumes the role of "a sociologist of literature" and observes that in the third-world context, the writers "must not stop at the stage of documenting social problems but move to the higher responsibility of proffering prescriptions." (161) The most vital part of the lecture is his piece of advice to the students (since the faculty in any case is incorrigible) wanting them to "Examine the condition of their lives because . . . the unexamined life is not worth living." Ikem as a poet and a novelist, like Achebe himself, is committed "to widen the scope of that self-examination." (158)

Answering a query after the lecture, Ikem casually reacts to the rumour about Sam's intention to have his image engraved on a coin. He remarks: "My view is that any serving President foolish enough to lay his head on a coin should know he is inciting people to take it off, the head I mean." (162) The Gazette under the leadership of a new editor flashed Ikem's lecture as the main story with a sensational caption: "EX-EDITOR ADVOCATES REGICIDE." (162)

In the final phase of the novel, Sam's regime turns fascist and resorts to violence indiscriminately. Ikem's residence is raided and ransacked at the dead of night; he is arrested; put in hand-cuffs and taken away from his place. An official announcement puts out a fabricated story that Ikem tried to snatch the gun from his escort and was shot fatally in the altercation. Even his dead body is not handed over to his friends for burial. This marks the fall of the first 'green bottle,' the victim of state-repression. Larry Diamond links up Ikem's murder to

> the real life-murder of Newswatch editor Dele Giwa in October 1986. Like the fictional Ikem Osodi, Dele Giwa was a hero to a great many of his countrymen, intellectuals and non-literates alike. Like Ikem, he was a crusader for freedom, accountability and justice, a brash investigator, a fearless and outspoken commentator . . the similarity between the two men in temperament and political stature, and the considerable suspicion and circumstantial evidence linking Nigeria's state security apparatus to Giwa's murder, leaves one with an eerie feeling of the way life, and death, imitate art.[2]

This is how imaginative literature often bears a close resemblance to life and mirrors the prevalent contemporary situation in authentic terms.

NOTES

1. Chinua Achebe, *Anthills of the Savannah* (London: Picador in association with William Heinemann, 1987).
2. Larry Diamond, Review Essay, "Fiction of Political Thought," *African Affairs*, Vol. 88, No. 352 (July 1989), p. 437.